Working Class
MYSTIC

Working Class
MYSTIC

A Spiritual Biography of
George Harrison

GARY TILLERY

Theosophical Publishing House
Wheaton, Illinois * Chennai, India

Quest Books
Theosophical Publishing House
P. O. Box 270
Wheaton, IL 60187-0270

www.questbooks.net

Cover image courtesy Bill Zygmant, www.billzygmant.co.uk
Cover design by Drew Stevens
Typesetting by Wordstop Technologies, Chennai, India

Library of Congress Cataloging-in-Publication Data

Tillery, Gary.
Working class mystic: a spiritual biography of George Harrison / Gary
Tillery.—1st Quest ed.
    p.   cm.
Includes bibliographical references and index.
ISBN 978-0-8356-0900-5
1. Harrison, George, 1943–2001. 2. Rock musicians—England—Biography.
3. Harrison, George, 1943–2001—Religion. I. Title.
ML420.H167T55 2011
782.42166092—dc22
[B]   2011015554

5 4 3 2 1 * 11 12 13 14 15

Printed in the United States of America

In memory of
my father,
B. M. Tillery

Contents

Author's Note

So much is lost when lyrics integrated into a background of carefully arranged and emotionally performed music are taken out of their proper context. In this book, in order to illustrate George Harrison's spiritual discoveries and development, I call attention to a range of key phrases from his songs. But I realize that they may seem fragmentary and uninspired when rendered on the page in stark black and white. The key songs addressed in the text are listed at the end of each major section of this book and you are encouraged to listen to them.

Acknowledgments

A work like this may appear to be purely the creation of an individual scouring the sources and then pounding away doggedly at the keyboard, but it would not be nearly as ready for the public without the benefit of scrutiny by objective eyes. I would like to express my gratitude to Seymour Shlaes for combing the first draft for errors and to Will Marsh for taking a jeweler's eye to text I considered ready for print. I would also be remiss if I didn't thank Quest Books, specifically Sharron Dorr, Nancy Grace, and Richard Smoley, for their input in making *Working Class Mystic* a worthy tribute to the "Quiet Beatle."

Introduction

One by one we get awakened by the sound of Krishna's flute. His flute works in many ways.

—George Harrison

I n the spring of 1965, when he accepted a long-standing dinner invitation, George Harrison had no reason to suspect that the trajectory of his religious life was about to change forever.

The son of a Roman Catholic mother and a lapsed Anglican father, Harrison had spent a decade in a long retreat from the spiritual teachings of his youth. Upon reaching an age when he felt comfortable emulating his father's avoidance of Sunday services, he too began to skip the bout with boredom. Impressive but outdated liturgies held no appeal for him. Like his sister and two older brothers before him, he drifted into an irreligious frame of mind, focusing instead on the usual preoccupations of teenagers as well as the band he and his friends Paul McCartney and John Lennon had formed. When, ultimately, the Beatles broke through to stratospheric success and stellar fame, he relished all the material world had to offer. Spiritual concerns didn't enter his mind.

Then, while the Beatles were filming *Help!* in London, Harrison and his girlfriend persuaded John Lennon and his wife to join them in accepting a dinner invitation from the Beatles' dentist. After dinner, without their knowledge, their host gave them all coffee laced with LSD. Harrison later described what happened: "My brain and my consciousness and my awareness were pushed so far out that the only way I could begin to describe it is like an astronaut on the moon, or in his spaceship, looking back at the Earth. I was looking back to the Earth from my awareness."[1]

What he encountered with his awareness pushed "so far out" came as a revelation. In the enrapturing clarity of an LSD experience he unexpectedly found God.

The full recognition of that discovery did not come to him until months later. That night in April 1965, he understood only that he was filled with a strange and powerful emotion. He recalled, "I felt in love, not with anything or anybody in particular, but with everything. Everything was perfect, in a perfect light, and I had an overwhelming desire to go around the club telling everybody how much I loved them—people I had never seen before."[2]

When, in time, he was able to look back objectively at the experience, he realized that in those amazing hours he had embraced—and been embraced by—the divine. His life would never be the same. That first step along a new path led to others. He discovered an affinity with faraway India. He befriended Ravi Shankar and studied the sitar. He took up yoga and began to chant. He studied meditation under the Maharishi Mahesh Yogi and supported the worldwide mission of Swami Prabhupada. He became a devotee of Hinduism, visiting its temples and sacred places and studying the writings of its holy men. He came to worship Krishna.

He worked hard to subdue his own ego and devoted great effort to understanding the truth hidden behind this waking dream he believed we inhabit. Once he learned to view the world through the eyes of a mystic, he vacillated between detachment from and attachment to it. He preferred to remain out of the spotlight, but his empathy for suffering people on the other side of the planet led him to spearhead the first rock-and-roll super-event for charity. He felt content with his own relationship with the deity, yet he had the urge to write songs intended to awaken the "sleeping" masses. Though he spent his life as one of the world's most famous men, he was always delighted to slip on overalls and work boots and join in manual labor around his properties.

When he passed out of the material world, succumbing to cancer at age fifty-eight, those who surrounded him in his final hours, besides his family, were ones who shared his spiritual beliefs—members of the International Society of Krishna Consciousness and his lifelong friend Ravi Shankar.

George Harrison lived a singular and fascinating life, yet he never lost connection with his roots. While he rubbed shoulders with the artistic luminaries, financial titans, and political leaders of the world, he remained a son of Liverpool. At ease with holy men discussing the wisdom of the Upanishads and the Bhagavad Gita, he was ever the down-to-earth bloke whose father drove a bus, whose brothers were tradesmen, and who had himself worked as an apprentice electrician at Blackler's until the day his destiny called.

John Lennon once called himself a working-class hero.

George Harrison was a working-class mystic.

Part One

LIVING IN THE MATERIAL WORLD

1

Liverpool

George Harrison was welcomed into the material world on February 24, 1943, arriving eighteen minutes before midnight in the upstairs bedroom of 12 Arnold Grove in Wavertree, a poor neighborhood in south Liverpool.

His father, Harold, and mother, Louise, had chosen to marry in the inauspicious year of 1930, seven months after the stock market crash. As the Great Depression gripped the planet, the family added a daughter, named after her mother, in 1931, and a son, named after his father, in 1934. A second son, Peter, came along while Hitler's Luftwaffe was attempting to pound the British into submission during the summer of 1940. George, the baby of the family, was born at the very turning point of World War II. England and the world had withstood the worst of the Fuehrer's crazed ambitions. Axis advances in the Caucasus, North Africa, and the Pacific had been blunted or repelled, and in America the "Arsenal of Democracy" began to build at a rate faster than the Axis powers could hope to match.

Harold H. Harrison had worked as a steward on ocean-going vessels—the same line of work pursued by John Lennon's father, Alfred. Unlike Freddie, Harry found the protracted absences from his wife unendurable. He turned his back on the seaman's life to seek a job in Liverpool. For fifteen months, in the depth of the Depression, he was unemployed. At last he found a position as a bus conductor, earning barely enough to eke out a living, but at least having the solace of seeing his family at the end of each day.

Liverpool had been a working-class town for centuries. As the best port on England's west coast, it had been the point of first contact for ocean-going commerce—the place sailors, traders, and travelers saw first. Raw materials from around the British Empire arrived at its docks, while manufactured goods were being shipped out. Factories sprang up to take advantage of the location, refining sugar, milling grain. Hardy men worked in them, many fresh immigrants. Liverpool was the site of England's first black population, Europe's first China Town, and, during the Great Famine of the mid-1800s, an influx of Irish that ultimately amounted to a quarter of the residents. In George Harrison's youth, Liverpool was a city of seamen, dock workers, factory hands, and tradesmen—the kind of people who could shrug off eighty air raids by the Luftwaffe and go back to work—tough, flinty, no-nonsense people who got things done.

Housing for blue-collar Liverpudlians was rudimentary. The ten-shilling-a-week home George grew up in was a simple brick house midway down an unbroken row of similar structures along an echoing cul-de-sac, a house composed of two hundred-square-foot bedrooms upstairs and an equal-sized living room and kitchen below. The front door opened directly onto the sidewalk. Visitors had merely to step across a raised threshold to be standing in the small living room. There they saw a small, seldom-used fireplace; beyond lay a small kitchen with an iron cooking stove and stairs leading to the two bedrooms. Out the back door, across a narrow paved yard, was the outhouse, and baths had to be taken in a zinc tub that hung on the wall outside when not in use.[1]

This house was Harrison's home for the first six years of his life, a time of bone-chilling awakenings on winter mornings—he'd often have to chip ice off the *inside* of the windows—but the warmth of familial relations among six individuals interacting in a cozy space.

Being the baby of the family, George was naturally the focus of all eyes. One of his earliest memories was from about the age of four. He recalled standing on a stool, singing a song titled "One Meat Ball" as his family surrounded him. He also enjoyed putting on puppet shows. He had a range of animal puppets and he would entertain his parents and siblings with improvised skits that made them laugh.[2]

Like his mother, George was baptized a Catholic, but as a result of the postwar baby boom primary schools were bulging with new students. When the time came for George to attend, the Harrisons decided to enroll him where there was sufficient room, at Dovedale Primary, a state-run school near Penny Lane.

Religion was not of central importance in the Harrison household. Harry had a northern workingman's suspicion of the church and did not attend services. George recalled: "Although they always say people who weren't Catholics were Church of England, he didn't appear to be anything." Harry's ambivalence influenced young George, who as a child accompanied his mother to Catholic masses, which she made sure to attend at least on major holidays. However, after celebrating his first Holy Communion at age eleven, he followed in his father's footsteps and never underwent confirmation. "I thought, 'I'm not going to bother with that, I'll just confirm it later myself.'"[3]

His sister, Louise, was also swayed for a time by her mother's wishes and went away to be educated at a convent school. Eventually, though, she shared George's disenchantment. She observed that as children they had both been ruled by fear—afraid they would burn in Hell if they didn't conform to the church's viewpoint. But later, as they grew up and became independent thinkers, they rebelled against the idea of a "crazy god" who was "zapping everybody with thunderbolts." They decided that such a god did not deserve their allegiance.[4]

Catholic ritual and dogma held no fascination for him, but Harrison as a child had mystical experiences. Unexpectedly, for no apparent reason, he would be overwhelmed by an odd sensation. His everyday perceptions would be superseded and he would begin to feel extremely tiny while simultaneously retaining a sense of his wholeness. As with all mystical experiences, the state was difficult to capture in words. "It was feeling like two different things at the same time. And this little thing, with this feeling that would vibrate right through me, would start off like rolling around and it would start getting bigger and bigger and faster and faster until it was going like so far and getting so fast that it was mind-boggling, and I'd come out of it really scared." As an adult, having experimented with mind-altering substances and meditation, he overcame his terror and learned to induce the state at will. During the *Abbey Road* sessions, he would slip off alone to a sound booth to repeat it.[5]

When Harrison started school at Dovedale another student was already there, two years ahead of him. The boy came from the more affluent suburb of Woolton and was someone George would later grow to idolize—an exceedingly bright but rebellious student named John Lennon.

George was a bright lad himself, and just like John Lennon he came to dislike the routine and the regimentation of school. Perhaps because he had grown accustomed to being indulged at home, perhaps because of his budding sense of individuality, he detested having to meet the expectations of the school authorities. Just like Lennon he responded with surliness, and his rebelliousness was met with frequent detentions and in the end disciplinary canings.[6]

In 1954, when George graduated from Dovedale and moved on to Liverpool Institute, his dislike of school graduated into hatred. He later wrote: "The whole idea of it was so serious. You can't smile and you are not allowed to do this or that. Be here, stand there, shut up, sit down." He found the environment inimical and responded by withdrawing both psychologically and physically. One of his teachers from those years, Arthur Evans, recalled him as an exceedingly quiet, even introverted boy who preferred to sit in the remotest part of the room and never even look up.[7]

The teachers at Liverpool Institute seemed to fall into one of two categories: old military veterans or recent graduates with no experience—neither group capable of making education interesting and both quick to turn to heavy-handed discipline. "It moulded us into being frightened. There was a rot which set in. They say that children will learn something if it is exciting, but when the rot sets in, you stop learning and being open to everything." Many teachers did not hesitate to browbeat their students and treated some of them with contempt. One teacher forced disobedient pupils to sit in the chair adjacent to a student notorious for his body odor. George found this behavior so deplorable that he deliberately sat next to the boy and befriended him.[8]

He shirked the work assigned to him and took to letting his hair grow shaggy and flouting the school dress code. He would keep his dark blazer buttoned during class to hide a canary yellow vest borrowed from his brother Harry. He used his mother's sewing machine to taper the legs of his trousers and started wearing shoes with pointed toes, emulating the fashion of Liverpool's tougher teens—known as Teddy Boys.[9]

Having decided as early as the age of twelve that he wanted nothing to do with the army, Harrison watched in mystification as the Institute's cadets marched back and forth outside on Monday and Wednesday afternoons. The sight seemed bizarre to him. Why was this strange activity going on at a place of education? He later likened his reaction to the feelings of the main character in a 1960s' television series: "I never could discover why these normal things were normal. They always seemed crazy to me: everyone acting 'normally' but it was so like *The Prisoner*. You never quite know what it is they are talking about."[10]

Completely averse to study, he was unprepared at age fifteen when the time came to try for his General Certificate of Education. Before he could take the exams he had first to pass three subjects in a "mock" GCE. He passed only one—art—and was held back to repeat his final year with the upcoming class. He devoted a total of only one hour to the renewed effort before ceasing to attend school at all. Instead, he passed the time at local movie houses. When judgment day came at the end of the school year, he returned to pick up his final report and a testimonial intended to advise employers of his strengths and capabilities. His teachers wrote candidly that they scarcely knew him, and his testimonial read, "I cannot tell you what his work is like because he has not done any." Harrison burned the documents before his parents could read them. At the age of sixteen, his formal education came to an end.[11]

Living in a working-class city as an uneducated youth without any trade or marketable skill, George was sliding toward an adult life spent on menial work for subsistence wages. He had only one passion, but that pointed to a career path more insecure than any of the others.

Just after his thirteenth birthday, in early 1956, George had begun to pal around with Irene, the seventeen-year-old girlfriend of his brother Harry. Harry had gone away to do his National Service, and for Irene, an only child, Harry's brother George resembled a younger brother. She, in turn, filled the role of George's sister, Louise, who had gone away to a teacher training college. Irene began to invite George to accompany her to musical shows at the Empire Theatre. One day they caught a performance by the current rage in England. His name was Lonnie Donegan, his specialty was skiffle—a British take on American folk tunes like "Rock Island Line" and "John Henry," delivered at a rollicking tempo—and his instrument was a guitar.

Within days George's mother noticed him sketching guitars on every piece of paper he could find. When a school friend offered to sell him a guitar for three pounds, he appealed to his mother for the money. She bought the instrument for him, never realizing what a life-altering event it would be for him. In the coming weeks and months, he made an arduous effort to learn to play. His brother Peter had taken up guitar at almost the same time. Together, like many other teenagers of the time, they formed a skiffle group of their own. They called themselves the Rebels and even secured a paying engagement at the nearby British Legion Club.[12]

Lonnie Donegan may have ignited the fire, but what fanned it into a blaze was the British discovery that year of a whole new style of music from "across the pond." Like many of the other restless youth of the time, Harrison felt bored by the bland popular music being played on the government-run BBC. What he loved, whenever the faint signal permitted, was the music coming from Radio Luxembourg, a station on the Continent that played the rock-and-roll hits sweeping America. One day George heard Elvis Presley singing "Heartbreak Hotel," and the tune "lodged itself permanently in the back of my brain." Elvis followed that with such rhythm-heavy, finger-snapping songs as "Blue Suede Shoes," "Hound Dog," and "Don't Be Cruel." Then in his wake came a barrage of infectious, up-tempo numbers from Little Richard, Buddy Holly, Chuck Berry, Jerry Lee Lewis, Carl Perkins, and others. Another revolution seemed to be taking place across the Atlantic, this time not political but cultural.

George diligently applied himself to learning his instrument by mimicking what he heard on Radio Luxembourg and studying the songs when he could obtain them on recordings. He convinced his mother to buy him a guitar of much higher quality for thirty pounds and worked to pay her back by delivering meat for a local butcher. To his delight, one of the customers had a son who had actually met Buddy Holly during his British tour. Better still, the boy had Buddy Holly records, and he lent them to George to listen to and study.[13]

Harrison's intense fascination with the guitar gave him something in common with another student attending Liverpool Institute—Paul McCartney. Riding the bus together for an hour each way every day gave them the opportunity to become acquainted, and even though Paul was almost a year older than George and a far more diligent student, they bonded in their mutual love of rock and roll.

Paul McCartney's fateful introduction to John Lennon took place on July 6, 1957, following a public performance by John's group, the Quarrymen. John, who went on to Quarry Bank High School after graduating from Dovedale, had formed his group in March. He had intended to play skiffle music, but because of his own love of the new sound from America he was in the process of transforming the group into a rock-and-roll band. When Paul walked onto the grounds of St. Peter's Church that summer afternoon and first heard the Quarrymen, John was singing "Come Go with Me," a Top Forty hit for the Del Vikings. After their show, the Quarrymen went indoors for a break before undertaking a second performance that evening. In the interim a mutual friend, Ivan Vaughan, introduced Paul to John. Paul impressed John with his prowess on the guitar and was subsequently invited to join John's band. That summer the two met at each other's houses, and their bond grew stronger that fall when John enrolled at Liverpool Art College, which was situated next door to Liverpool Institute. McCartney finally joined the Quarrymen in a professional engagement on October 18.

In March 1958, Paul brought his friend George along to meet the band at a house in Old Roan, a suburb northeast of Liverpool. Colin Hanton, drummer for the Quarrymen, remembered: "It was at a club we used to go to, called the Morgue. It was in the cellar of this big old derelict house. No bar or coffee or anything, just a cellar with dark rooms off it, and one big blue light bulb sticking out of the wall." At Paul's prompting, George performed "Guitar Boogie Shuffle" as well as the hypnotic riff from a popular instrumental titled "Raunchy." While he wasn't invited to join the band right away, he had established his credentials. From then on he was welcome to show up at Quarrymen performances and be on hand to substitute if one of the other guitarists failed to arrive.[14]

Harrison's persistence was eventually rewarded. His personality and ability meshed so well with Lennon and McCartney that they decided he should replace Eric Griffiths, one of the founding members of the group. The band scheduled a practice at Paul's house without informing Griffiths. When Griffiths got word of what was happening and phoned there, John and Paul deputized his best friend in the group, Colin Hanton, to deliver the unpleasant news.

Real tragedy struck on July 15, 1958. John Lennon's mother stepped in front of a speeding car and died instantly. A member of the Quarrymen, Nigel Whalley, chanced to witness the accident. Moments after walking away from a conversation with her, he heard the squeal of brakes from the highway. He turned back to see her body hurling through the air.[15]

Though John had not lived with her since the age of five—he was raised instead by his Aunt Mimi—the loss was especially bitter because he had recently reestablished contact and his mother was supportive of his musical dreams. He turned his despair outward, directing his anger and venomous humor on the world. Paul McCartney could relate to John's pain. He had lost his own mother in October 1956, when she suffered an embolism following a mastectomy for cancer. George, spared such trauma as a teenager, could only imagine how his friends felt. Both of his parents would survive until the decade of the seventies.

George idolized John Lennon, attracted by his self-assurance, drive to succeed, irreverence, and wit. He seized on John as a role model and treasured the time spent in his presence. Though more private than shy, George had not yet begun serious dating. He was therefore unaware of how much of a nuisance he might be. He would spot John slipping away off campus in the company of his girlfriend and future wife, Cynthia, and hail them from behind with a whistle. Intent on spending time together somewhere, they would turn to find the eager boy hurrying to catch them, looking for companionship. "Where are you two off to? Can I come?" Often, when Cynthia prevailed on John to take her to a film, George would be sitting on John's other side.[16]

Throughout 1958 and 1959, the band continued to struggle on from gig to gig, for a time under the new name of Johnny and the Moondogs, later as the Silver Beatles.

In mid-1959, George left school after burning the records of his failure. Just sixteen, he lived for months on sporadic income from occasional bookings and vague dreams that the band would succeed. With increasing embarrassment, he borrowed money from his father, who finally prodded him one day, "Don't you think you'd better get a job?" George applied with the city, but couldn't pass the test. Finally he checked at the Youth Employment Centre, where someone told him that Blackler's department store had a position open. When he went there the position had already been filled, but he was directed to another department, where he was hired as an apprentice electrician. He

15

was paid a pittance and did little more than odd jobs, but his father saw it as a promising start. He gave George a set of electrician's screwdrivers as a Christmas present.[17]

At last the band caught a break. John Lennon had pressured an artist friend of his, Stuart Sutcliffe, to purchase a bass and join the band. Sutcliffe had no musical talent, but he had an acquaintance, Allan Williams, who appreciated the group's verve and looked past their roughness and began booking them into his coffee bar, the Jacaranda. Williams was also a promoter, and in May 1960 he arranged for the Silver Beatles to provide backup for a vocalist who went by the stage name of Johnny Gentle. They were to accompany him on a two-week tour of Scotland. Convinced that they were at last about to succeed professionally, Harrison went to his boss at Blackler's and resigned.[18]

Shortly afterward one of the Jacaranda's most popular acts, a Caribbean steel band, abruptly and mysteriously left town. When Williams investigated, he learned that they had been lured away by a nightclub in faraway Hamburg, Germany. Mystified, but smelling the scent of opportunity, Williams journeyed to Hamburg to see for himself what had motivated the band's departure. He discovered a thriving nightclub scene and soon positioned himself as an intermediary to scout out talent in England. In August 1960, on behalf of Bruno Koschmider, who owned two clubs in the St. Pauli district of Hamburg, Williams arranged a paying engagement for the newly renamed Beatles that would transform their music and their lives.[19]

Harrison, still a boy of only seventeen, appealed to his parents to let him take advantage of the opportunity. His father was skeptical. George's two older brothers had solid work as tradesmen—one a mechanic, the other a welder. To his working-class mind, they were on the pathway to successful lives. Playing music in a band was a hobby, not a career. Louise Harrison, however, was more understanding. The boy was still young. Why not let him pursue his dreams before he settled down?[20]

Knowing only that he felt the call of something indefinable, George left the nest and struck off for the Continent.

2

Freedom

In 1960, the St. Pauli district of Hamburg represented the polar opposite of spirituality—the Sodom and Gomorrah George had heard about as a child from clergymen in negative yet tantalizing tones. Gamblers, strippers, pimps, male and female prostitutes, gays, transvestites, mud wrestlers, drug peddlers—all consorted and intermingled in a whirlpool of iniquity. Alcoholics, gangsters, and off-duty seamen rubbed shoulders with decadent businessmen and bohemian university students. The setting was custom-made for the Devil's music—rock and roll—and Herr Koschmider welcomed the Beatles to a club that was to become their own little corner of Gomorrah. He had named it the Indra—ironic in view of the role Indian culture would play in Harrison's life. The chief god of the Rig Veda, the oldest of India's holy texts, Indra was forever striving to defeat the forces of darkness.[1]

The main avenue through the St. Pauli district was the Reeperbahn, a boisterous corridor of neon lights, blaring music, and signs touting "Girls! Girls! Girls!" Off this main artery branched a cobblestone street called Grosse Freiheit (Great Freedom), which, as one ventured farther from the Reeperbahn, grew increasingly less boisterous. Beyond Koschmider's larger and more successful club, the Kaiserkeller, near the dismal end of the Grosse Freiheit, down a flight of stairs, Bruno led the bright-eyed lads from Liverpool to their new home, the Indra.

The tiny former strip club had a funereal atmosphere. No band was playing on the small stage. The jukebox sat silent. Only two forlorn customers glanced up at them. Koschmider blustered, "No one comes to this place. But you'll make it go when you make show." He led them back up the stairs, outside again, toward the place where they would be staying. Still farther down the street, past a cinema called the Bambi Kino, which showed old Westerns and an occasional porno film, they turned a corner and walked to the back of the building.

They entered a door, passed through a pitch-black corridor, and arrived at last at a barren room lit by a single bulb, a room in which most of the space was occupied by two single beds and a sofa. George saw John Lennon, first in line, claim one of the beds, and Stu Sutcliffe, right behind him, the other. He quickly staked out the sofa for himself. McCartney and Pete Best—the drummer they had recruited the day before leaving for Hamburg—stared at each other, wondering if they were expected to sleep on the floor. Koschmider reassured them that there were two more bedrooms. Some twenty-five yards farther along the corridor, adjacent to the women's lavatory for the Bambi Kino, they were shown two closet-like rooms. Neither had any sort of lighting. To see, even in the daytime, McCartney and Best would need to use flashlights or strike matches. Each of the rooms measured about five feet by six feet, and most of that space was filled by a single bed. McCartney observed of his, "You could just about swing a cat in here—provided it's got no tail."

"Only temporary, only temporary," Koschmider kept promising—a promise that would never be fulfilled.[2]

The band quickly learned what Koschmider meant by "make show." He had not hired them to stand on the stage like professionals and perform their music with dignity. The Indra's customers paid dearly for their drinks, and they expected to be *entertained*. "Make show" meant keep moving, jump around, cavort, make a fool of yourself.

The Beatles began to make show for seven hours a night. John and Paul were the most unrestrained, learning there was no limit to what they might do—short of killing the patrons. While performing their numbers they would smoke, drink, eat, joke, make faces, shout at each other and the audience, feign fights, lie on the floor while continuing to play their instruments, and plunge into the crowd to dance or jump around. Taking excessive doses of Preludin, a stimulant legal at the time but subsequently banned, John soon passed beyond unrestrained and turned maniacal, imitating a hunchback, flinging the microphone into the air, leaping offstage to do splits on the dance floor, returning from a break without pants and with a toilet seat lodged around his neck. He resented having to act like a performing monkey and vented his anger by shouting "Seig heil!" and "Where's your tank?" and "Get up and dance, you lazy bastards!" George would get caught up in the antics—jostling with John and Paul and feigning anger when one hopped on the other's back and they came crashing into him or when John threw something at him—but mainly he considered it his duty to focus on his guitar and keep the music flowing. Throughout the craziness, Stu Sutcliffe did his best to emulate James Dean, wearing sunglasses no matter how dark the room, and often turning his back to the audience—a stance that served to hide his amateurish finger work on the bass.

Their audiences were just as unruly as the band—and so quick to start fights that the waiters and barmen all carried truncheons and tear gas. George recalled, "They would have fights and beat the hell out of each other and then the bad guy would get thrown out of the back door, and so an hour later he'd come back with reinforcements and then it was really wicked—blood everywhere. . . . Inevitably it ended in blood and tears. And tears for the band, too, with the gas in our faces."[3]

One fringe benefit of the hellacious, seven-night-a-week schedule was the ample supply of women. Girls would constantly send drinks up for the band, or at least their favorite member, and they were eager to be approached during breaks and after the show. Despite working for slave wages and living in "humble dungeons," as Pete Best called their quarters, the Beatles enjoyed having two or three women a night each and often traded them between one another as the night progressed. They eventually learned that many of their admirers were "working girls," prostitutes who didn't mind giving for free what they were paid for during their own workday. Many worked in the Herbertstrasse, a street about which the Beatles kept hearing tantalizing stories.

The five soon decided to explore St. Pauli and seek out this El Dorado of vice. They found the strange street only five minutes away. Tall barriers at both ends blocked the entire corridor from the view of passersby. To gain access, visitors had to go through an L-shaped passage. Arriving in front of the barrier, George was embarrassed to find an official notice warning that no one below the age of eighteen was permitted to enter. He would not be eighteen for another six months and was in fact already breaking the law every night he spent in St. Pauli. At ten o'clock each night the police fanned out across the district, checking everyone's identification to be sure no one under the age of eighteen remained. Allan Williams had blustered so effectively when the Beatles arrived at the German border that they had been passed through without proper documents. Because they were foreigners, the Hamburg police did not scrutinize them as closely as native citizens. The band members were assumed to be at least eighteen or they would not be there.

All of the other Beatles were at least that age, and as they stood at the gateway to sin, they began to tease George. John Lennon held him back by the arm: "No George, you can't come in with us *men*." The other four chimed in, "You're still only a baby!" After sufficient teasing, they strolled into the forbidden street and discovered a supermarket of sex and perversion. Decorating doorways and windowsills, a host of lovely women struck various poses, revealing generous amounts of skin. The entire block was one cavalcade of carnality. An especially memorable sight was a tall, extremely well-endowed woman wearing thigh-high boots and wielding a whip. As they walked farther, they recognized a girl who had visited them in the rear of the Bambi Kino. She waved and invited them to come inside "for free!" The five began to make regular passes through the Herbertstrasse on the way to have English-style breakfasts at the Seaman's Mission by the quayside, even though the detour added to the length of their walk.[4]

The Beatles and Koschmider had a written agreement for a two-month engagement at the Indra, renewable by mutual consent. Shortly before that period ended, the officials closed the Indra on October 4 because neighbors had been complaining about the noise level. Delighted by the crowds the Beatles had started to draw, Koschmider immediately transferred them to his larger club, the Kaiserkeller. There they alternated performances with another band from Liverpool, Rory Storm and the Hurricanes. They renewed their contract on October 16 and kept up their frenetic lifestyle into November.[5]

One night a magazine illustrator named Klaus Voormann strolled in and caught their performance. Following an argument with his girlfriend, Astrid Kirchherr, he had escaped to the streets, but finding them cold and damp, he finally decided to take solace in St. Pauli's nightlife. After hearing the Beatles play and witnessing the excitement they generated, he persuaded Astrid to come and see for herself. In short order, they and their circle of friends became good friends with the group. Astrid was especially taken with Stuart Sutcliffe. Though neither spoke the other's language, the two were soon engaged to be married, and Astrid convinced her mother to allow Stuart to move into a room in their house.[6]

The Beatles' first visit to Hamburg lasted only slightly more than a hundred days, but they were days packed with learning experiences. Harrison would later look back on the time with mixed emotions, aghast at the squalor of their living conditions but grateful for the dramatic improvement of his skills and professionalism. Another benefit was the brief hint of success—of discovering that it was possible to do what he truly wanted to do and be compensated for it, even if that first compensation was barely a living wage.

An even-greater benefit the experience gave him was a taste of pure freedom. Like any seventeen-year-old moving out from under the watchful eyes of his parents, he had been compelled to make his own choices and develop his personal survival skills. However, even more significant, he was thrown into a milieu in which the usual constraints of civilization did not apply. St. Pauli pushed him all the way down the road of freedom to reveal what lay at the end—a world in which all passions were indulged and debauchery was commonplace. Still in thrall to his hormones, he saw the allure but not the tragedy. In the next few years, as he rose to the pinnacle of the material world and savored life as one of its most famous and admired men, he would discover the truth: what seemed so desirable was actually an illusion. For now, he knew only that the taste of freedom set him apart from the friends he had left back in Liverpool. Their lives had near horizons—finish school, choose a mate, find a trade, go to work, bring home your check, indulge yourself at the cinema or public house on Saturday, drop in at church on Sunday if you felt so inclined. How could he ever settle for that life again?

The end came when the Beatles outgrew Bruno Koschmider. In off-hours they liked to visit other clubs, to listen to and meet their competition. In the more elegant Top Ten Club they befriended another English performer, Tony Sheridan. He invited the Beatles to jam with his back-up group, the Jets. This violated a clause in the Beatles' contract, which stated they could not play in another venue within twenty-five miles of the Indra. When the owner of the Top Ten heard them playing and made them an offer to switch to his club for more money, they leaped at the chance. They felt no loyalty to Koschmider, who had treated them like trained monkeys and conveniently forgotten his breezy promises.[7]

Koschmider saw things differently. He was furious at the prospect of losing the band he had made stars. He retaliated by informing the police that Harrison was underage and working in Germany illegally. George was ordered out of the country on November 21, and his bandmates were forced to say good-bye to their lead guitarist. For another week they continued to play at the Kaiserkeller. Then, at the end of November, they decided to pack up their belongings and move secretly to the dormitory where Tony Sheridan lived. Lennon made a quick and clean getaway, but when McCartney and Best slipped into their "humble dungeons" and began gathering their personal effects, they were hampered by the lack of light. They improvised, pinning four flammable prophylactics to the wall of the corridor outside their rooms and igniting them. While the burning rubber flickered and gave off an odious smell, they succeeded in packing and made their getaway too. In their haste, they paid no heed when the burning condoms scorched the old tapestry covering the walls. Two days later, Paul and Pete were rousted from their bunks in the new dormitory by police, who charged them with setting a fire in the Bambi Kino. They were hustled to a police station and booked, spent a few hours in jail, then were placed on a flight to England at German expense, not even permitted to return to their room and gather their belongings. His mates scattered to the winds, Lennon soon followed them home to Liverpool.[8]

For a few weeks, the Beatles hibernated. Harrison roamed the icy winter streets without direction. Should he slink back to Blackler's and ask for his old job? Should he look for other work? He had no way to know it at the time, but the band had reached its nadir; a winding yellow brick road to the top was about to appear.

Once they put out word they were back in town, the Beatles succeeded in getting two minor bookings in mid-December. Then, on December 27, 1960, a local disc jockey and emcee, Bob Wooler, arranged for them to play at Litherland Town Hall—an event that would prove pivotal in their career. Wooler was impressed by the dynamic stage presence the Beatles had developed in Germany, as well as by their rough-and-tumble look. With no one to please but themselves, they had let their hair grow and taken to wearing jackets and pants made of black leather. He expected them to make a striking impression.

He promoted them in the local newspaper by relying on the cachet of their experience on the Continent: "Direct from Hamburg!" Readying them to go on that night, Wooler caught Paul McCartney's attention and emphasized, "As soon as I announce you, go straight into the first number." When the time came and the curtains parted, he began, "Direct from Hamburg!" Paul took that as his cue to scream "I'M GONNA TELL AUNT MARY 'BOUT UNCLE JOHN!" and the group exploded into "Long Tall Sally"—delivering the song with the pile-driver intensity they had perfected on the Grosse Freiheit over the din of rowdy customers. Few people in that part of north Liverpool were familiar with the Beatles. Staggered by a sound like none they had heard before, and seeing the strange bunch of scruffy, leather-clad musicians, most of the audience assumed they were listening to some exotic group from Germany taking rock and roll to electrifying new heights. The room erupted. Teenagers rushed the stage. Dancers lost themselves in a frenzy. After the show those fans who met with the Beatles expressed amazement that they spoke such good English.[9]

Wooler worked regularly at the Cavern, a fruit and vegetable warehouse in downtown Liverpool that had been converted into a music venue. After witnessing the reaction to the Beatles at Litherland Town Hall, he persuaded the Cavern's owner to let them perform for lunchtime crowds. On February 9, 1961, they performed there for the first time, beginning an association that would last until August 1963. The audience ate up the raucous displays of rock and roll, and John and Paul—who knew how to "make show," were only too happy to entertain them. George continued to concentrate on his playing, which cemented his reputation as "the quiet one." He stepped into the foreground only for his guitar solos and such numbers as "Sheik of Araby" and Buddy Holly's "Crying, Waiting, Hoping," for which he sang lead.

In April 1961 the band returned to Hamburg. This time they went with proper papers, and this time they went directly to the Top Ten Club. During the visit, Harrison, by happenstance, helped to create the hairstyle that would soon become the Beatles' trademark and by mid-decade would be imitated by men throughout the Western world. Previously, like the typical rockers of their time, the boys had combed their hair up in front and swept back along the sides—using Vaseline, if necessary, to keep it fixed into place. One day George accompanied Astrid Kirchherr and Klaus Voormann to nearby baths for a swim. When he emerged from the water, his wet hair naturally hung down across his forehead. It resisted combing upward and he had no Vaseline available. Both Astrid and Klaus told him not to bother—that it looked very good the way it was. He thought, "Well, these people are cool—if *they* think it's good, I'll leave it like this." His hair dried naturally down and he left it. John and Paul would soon change their styles, too, during a visit to

Paris that fall, when they met up with a friend of Astrid and Klaus who wore his hair in a similar fashion. The style quickly became associated with the Beatles.[10]

Once more they worked with Tony Sheridan, and as a result of their relationship with him they recorded professionally for the first time. A German music publisher came in one night, witnessed Sheridan and the Beatles playing, and later recommended them to a friend, Bert Kaempfert. In late June, just before they ended their engagement in Hamburg and returned to Liverpool, Kaempfert arranged for a session and recorded a total of seven songs—five with the band backing Sheridan, two on its own. Their two songs were "Ain't She Sweet," with John Lennon singing the lead, and an instrumental titled "Cry for a Shadow." Harrison had written the latter with Lennon while they were attempting to play a song neither knew well—a song performed by a Liverpool band named the Shadows. "Cry for a Shadow" became the first song written by the Beatles to be professionally recorded.[11]

The session with Kaempfert was to play a key role in the discovery and ultimate success of the Beatles. One of the songs with Tony Sheridan as front man, "My Bonnie," was released in Germany and reached number five in the charts. Stu Sutcliffe, who now lived in Hamburg with Astrid Kirchherr, sent copies of the disc to the band. One of these copies ended up in the hands of Bob Wooler, who began to play and promote it at every opportunity. On October 28, 1961, a fan who had heard Wooler touting the record walked into a shop owned by Brian Epstein and requested a copy. Epstein had never heard of the record, but agreed to fill the fan's order. Only after some research did he learn that the German mystery group behind Sheridan was, in truth, the Beatles, who were packing in crowds every weekday only a few blocks from his shop. (Adding to the confusion, the German record company had altered the band's name to "the Beat Brothers" because "the Beatles" sounded like *die pedels*—north German slang, equivalent to "the Pricks.")[12]

Epstein first went to see the Beatles on November 9, 1961, and was captivated by the band and the audience reaction they stirred. On

Sunday, December 3, he proposed to become their manager. Though they had not yet signed a contract with him, Epstein secured an audition for the Beatles with Decca Records, in London, on January 1, 1962. This they failed, possibly because Epstein insisted on selecting the music he thought they should play, but more likely because the Decca executives failed to perceive the diamond in the rough. Epstein kept trying with other labels and in mid-February succeeded in meeting with the A&R (artists and repertoire) man for Parlophone—a label owned by EMI—a dapper, well-spoken gentleman named George Martin. Listening to the 78-rpm demos Epstein had brought along to the Abbey Road studios, Martin complimented Harrison's guitar playing and Paul's voice and expressed modest interest in the group. He said he would consider listening to more, but without offering a timeline.[13]

In April 1962, the Beatles went to Hamburg for a third time, booked for seven weeks into the Star Club. John, Paul, and Pete flew into Hamburg on April 11 (George, because of illness, went the following day) and were met at the airport by a devastated Astrid Kirchherr. Stuart Sutcliffe, only twenty-one, had died suddenly the day before of a brain hemorrhage after falling down some stairs. In spite of the blow, they began their contracted performances on Friday, April 13. Epstein, who had accompanied Harrison, attended some business meetings and returned to England to continue his uphill struggle to gain the group proper recognition. On May 9, at 11:30 a.m., he met once more with George Martin, and an hour later he sent the telegram the Beatles had been longing to receive: "Congratulations boys. EMI request recording session. Please rehearse new material."

The band flew back to Liverpool on June 2 and prepared for the all-important session—set for June 6—at which they would meet the man who could make or break their dreams. Now the hundreds of nights they had spent charming tough crowds paid off. In what was customarily a nerve-wracking situation, they displayed self-confident camaraderie. George Martin began the session elsewhere but came in when one of the engineers thought he should hear "Love Me Do." Even more than their music, Martin was impressed by the Beatles' group chemistry and sense of humor. Of a number of songs they auditioned, he chose four to record. Afterward, like a master summoning his pupils, he called them upstairs to his control booth to listen to the replay. Trying to put them at ease, he invited them to speak up if there was anything at all they would like to change—saying that he would try to put it right. "Well, for a start," said Harrison, "I don't like your tie." The impudence might have irked a typical record executive, but Martin had produced records for Peter Sellers and Spike Milligan. Amused by George's wisecrack, he bonded with the group.[14]

Only the taciturn Pete Best did not hit it off with George Martin, and in Martin's opinion his drumming skills were not adequate for recording purposes. Martin candidly informed Brian Epstein of the fact. The other three Beatles had been mulling a change of drummer for some time. Harrison had actively lobbied for Ringo Starr, who had filled in for Best on occasion. "I conspired to get Ringo in for good; I talked to Paul and John until they came round to the idea." Seizing the opportunity, George went to Ringo's home to talk with him. Ringo was out of town, but George sat down to tea with his mother and told her that the Beatles wanted her son to be part of their group. Mrs. Starkey agreed to have Richie call them when he next phoned her. Once Ringo had accepted their offer, they asked Epstein to perform the dirty work of firing Best. The new lineup returned to the Abbey Road recording studio on September 4 and September 11, and the end result was released on October 5, 1962. The Beatles' first single was "Love Me Do" backed with "P.S. I Love You." On December 27, the record peaked at number seventeen on the British pop charts and the Beatles' rise to fame began.[15]

The following month their second single, "Please Please Me," was released. Immediate favorable reaction to the song begged the creation of an album to capitalize on the marketing opportunity. George Martin wanted to record the band live at the Cavern, but the acoustics proved so terrible that he changed his mind. The Beatles visited Abbey Road on February 11 and recorded the album in one ten-hour session. George sang lead on two songs—"Chains" and "Do You Want to Know a Secret." Eleven days later "Please Please Me" finally reached first place on the British charts, and on March 22 their first LP, also titled *Please Please Me*, was released. It became the best-selling album in Britain for thirty straight weeks. Soon the Beatles' already busy schedule became frantic as Epstein took advantage of the band being The Big New Thing. They went from concert gigs to performances on radio and television shows, and ran from photo sessions to magazine and newspaper interviews. Meanwhile, they were coming up with, arranging, and recording new songs.[16]

At first the songwriting team of Lennon and McCartney provided all of the original material the Beatles recorded. George Harrison's only foray into writing had been the simple instrumental he and Lennon had composed for fun, "Cry for a Shadow," and an even earlier and more amateurish ditty he created with Paul McCartney, "In Spite of All the Danger." In August 1963, while sick in bed in a hotel room in Bournemouth, England, George amused himself by trying to see if he could write a tune for the group. The title, fitting in view of Harrison's lifelong penchant for privacy, was "Don't Bother Me." They recorded the song on September 11 and 12, and included it on their second LP, *With the Beatles*.[17]

By the end of 1963, the Beatles had their own national radio show, their airport arrivals were being met by crowds of hysterical teenagers, American news media were beginning to report their impact, they were invited to a Royal Command Performance for the Queen Mother and Princess Margaret, their record "I Want to Hold Your Hand" became a million-seller even before its release, and a word was coined specifically to describe the frenzy surrounding them.[18]

In mid-September, just before "Beatlemania" began, Brian Epstein managed to schedule a short break for the four. Harrison traveled to the United States with his brother Peter to visit their sister, Louise. She had emigrated in 1954 and in early 1963 had moved with her family to a small town in southern Illinois. Although, by coincidence, "She Loves

You" was released by a small American label on the day George arrived, the Beatles were still a British phenomenon and relatively unknown in the United States. For two tranquil weeks George was free to come and go as he would never be again. The only stir he caused was the result of his hairstyle. A member of a local rock band who escorted him around town recalled, "I'd never seen any man with so much hair. Everywhere we went, people stared at him."[19]

What catapulted the Beatles to worldwide fame was their ballyhooed arrival in New York City on February 5, 1964, followed two nights later by their appearance on *The Ed Sullivan Show*. Some seventy-four million viewers tuned in to the broadcast—four out of ten Americans. From that week forward, the band achieved a level of fame no entertainer has enjoyed before or since. Even "the Quiet Beatle" became one of the most instantly recognized and intensely watched celebrities in the world.

Less than a month later they started work on a feature-length film. *A Hard Day's Night* began filming on March 2, 1964, under a tight schedule in order to have it ready for summer release. Of the four Beatles, Ringo impressed film reviewers the most, being featured in several comedic situations and carrying them off with aplomb. But Harrison also shone. Screenwriter Alun Owen wrote a scene tailor-made for his reticent personality and wry humor, lampooning the teen market, revealing the crassness of those who made a living off its desires and insecurities.

Filming had scarcely begun when Harrison became smitten with a pretty blonde model who portrayed a schoolgirl on a train. Her name was Pattie Boyd. The movie's director, Richard Lester, had worked with her previously in a television commercial, where she played the Smith's Crisp Girl and delightedly ate potato chips from a bag. She and George were seated next to each other at lunch, but exchanged only a few words. Pattie, although too painfully shy to speak, called the experience "electrifying." As the day's filming came to an end, George finally approached her and made clear his interest. Disconcertingly, he asked, "Will you marry me?" Not knowing how to answer, she laughed instead.

"Well," he said, "if you won't marry me, will you have dinner with me tonight?" Already in a steady relationship, Pattie nervously turned him down. By the time she returned to the set, on March 12, she had ended the relationship. When Harrison asked her again she accepted and soon became an integral part of his life. At Easter she accompanied him on a jaunt to Ireland, and in early May she and George vacationed in Tahiti with John Lennon and his wife, Cynthia.

For Pattie, the experience was like being caught up in a whirlwind and transported to some magical realm. The product of a broken home, with a cool, neglectful mother and a stern, disciplinarian stepfather, she had spent much of her childhood in the care of her grandparents and a nanny in Kenya. After returning to England in the late fifties, she had started work in a beauty salon and finally been saved from a hum-drum life by her natural beauty and intensely blue eyes. A salon patron who worked for a fashion magazine one day suggested that she would make a good model and invited her to come in for a professional photo session. That started her on the path that would lead to the meeting with Dick Lester and would encourage her personality to flower. Cynthia Lennon likened Pattie to a "very beautiful flimsy butterfly" and described her as "a friendly bubbly character, a great girl full of fun and boundless enthusiasm, very childlike but in no way immature." She found Pattie's London sophistication a soothing influence on Harrison's "northern bluntness."[20]

The year 1963 had witnessed the launch of Beatlemania in Great Britain; in 1964 the Beatles reached orbit worldwide. Their records dominated the international pop charts to a degree that has never been equaled. In March, preorders in Britain for their new song, "Can't Buy Me Love," exceeded a million copies. The number in the United States was 2.1 million. By April, the five best-selling singles in the United States were *all* by the Beatles. In Australia, that number was *six*. The frenetic pace at which they had been living for a year accelerated, with almost every day a blur of hotel rooms, limousines, airports, concerts, interviews, photo sessions, filming, recording, and radio and television appearances, interrupted by stolen moments spent working on new songs, all against a backdrop of screaming and grasping fans. For George, the daily grind was torture. He wrote Pattie that the only place he could find sanctuary was locked in the bathroom of his hotel room.[21]

In August the Beatles toured the United States, giving thirty-two performances in twenty-four cities in thirty-four days. On August 28, Bob Dylan slipped up to their room at New York's Delmonico Hotel, and all four met him for the first time. Dylan was particularly keen on meeting Lennon, the writer-artist-intellectual of the group, but the deepest and longest-lasting bond begun that night was with George Harrison. Their two reclusive personalities meshed, and as the years went by Harrison and Dylan would build a friendship, collaborate on songs, and even form a band together.

After introductions and pleasantries, Dylan pulled the four aside to let them know that he had brought with him a bag of marijuana. He had mistakenly assumed that they used it themselves. Learning that they hadn't, he drew them away into a closed room and rolled a joint for them to try. The experience changed them all in a profound way. They had used artificial stimulants since their first days in Hamburg, a necessary evil to make possible their energy-draining performances and decadent lifestyle. But they had never experienced anything resembling the soothing "high" of marijuana, the altered body chemistry that made the world seem simultaneously beautiful, worthy of love, and hilarious. They came away from the experience mellowed and, prompted by their altered perceptions, began to listen to music through new ears. George managed to get some marijuana before his return home and shared it with Pattie upon his arrival. Along with the other Beatles, he began to smoke it regularly.[22]

The influence of marijuana likely played a role in Harrison's aroused creativity as 1965 began. His sole contribution to the Beatles' songwriting so far had been "Don't Bother Me," written in August 1963. As Lennon and McCartney began to write songs for the second Beatles movie—*Help!*—George suddenly came up with two tunes, "I Need You" and "You Like Me Too Much." The band soon recorded them in mid-February, just before departing London for New Providence Island in the Bahamas, where filming was to begin.

No other year in George Harrison's life would prove more pivotal than 1965. As he turned twenty-two in a tropical paradise, he stood at the pinnacle of the material world—one of the world's best-loved celebrities, star of stage, screen, radio, and television, a man amassing wealth at a blistering pace, renowned for his musical skills, courted by the crème de la crème of society, about to receive a coveted honor from the monarch of the realm. He was living the existence he had daydreamed about as a working-class teenager in Liverpool. Yet the direction of his life was about to change radically. He was about to conclude that, contrary to the evidence of his senses, the world around him was not what it seemed—that it was, in fact, an illusion. Further, to begin to distinguish what was real from what was illusory, he was going to have to learn from the masters of an ancient and exotic land. Further still, and most challenging, he was going to have to change himself.

Full realization of all this was still more than a year away—a year filled with controversy and anxiety. Harrison would be forced during that time to reconsider the norms of his culture. In the end, he would realize that the material world was unsatisfying. He would find that, for him, there was only one road to contentment. He had to follow the path of mysticism.

3

The Final Tour

The first vague foreshadowing of George Harrison's new direction came as the Beatles began work in the Bahamas on *Help!* On February 25, 1965, they were being filmed riding bicycles around the island roads. While engaged in his morning meditation nearby, Swami Vishnu-devananda felt an urge to make contact with them. When he found them during a break from filming, he presented each with a copy of his book *The Complete Illustrated Book of Yoga*. George had no interest in it at the time, but years later—after visiting Rishikesh with the Maharishi—he delved into it and was surprised to learn that the Swami had come from Rishikesh. "I know it was part of a pattern," he said. "It was all planned that I should read it now. It all follows a path, just like our path. John, Paul, and George converged, then a little later Ringo. We were part of that action which led to the next reaction. We're all just little cogs in an action which everyone is part of."[1]

In April, filming of *Help!* shifted to London. To spice up one scene set in an Indian restaurant, a group of Indian musicians was hired to play in the background. One of the musicians cradled and plucked a sitar, and George found himself captivated. Perhaps it was simply a case of a musician intrigued by a new sound, but for Harrison the attraction was likely more deep-seated. During the winter of 1943, when he was still happily adrift in Louise Harrison's womb, his mother had enjoyed listening to the radio while she went about her housework. Her favorite program was a Sunday broadcast that featured music from "the jewel of the empire"—a program titled *Radio India*.[2]

Whatever the reason, Harrison found himself enchanted by the instrument. In August, during a stop in Los Angeles while the Beatles toured America, he mentioned his fascination to David Crosby and Roger McGuinn of the Byrds. As chance would have it, the foremost master of sitar, Ravi Shankar, recorded in the same studio they used. They played Harrison some of his records, and he conceived the idea of one day meeting Shankar. When he returned to England, George purchased a sitar of his own. He would use it, albeit in an elementary way, to add an air of mystery to John Lennon's "Norwegian Wood (This Bird Has Flown)." As his skills improved, he wrote "Love You To" specifically to showcase the exotic sound of the instrument.

The American tour in mid-1965 was not one the Beatles undertook gladly. The memory of 1964 was still fresh in mind: performing thirty-two shows in thirty-four days across a vast continent; making a hairbreadth escape as nine thousand fans crashed through an airport fence toward them; having their mobile dressing room overturned by zealots; riding an aircraft an astrologer predicted would crash with no survivors; playing in Las Vegas despite a bomb threat; facing the same inane questions at every press conference in every new city; meeting streams of mayors, councilmen, business leaders, and celebrities whose names they had never heard; having physically and mentally stricken children shoved at them in hopes their messianic aura would somehow be curative; spending day after day barricaded in their hotel rooms eating meals ordered through room service.[3]

The first concert in the 1965 tour set the tone for all the rest. Fifty-five thousand fans jammed into Shea Stadium—seeing the Beatles but not hearing them. From the moment the four arrived onstage, they were assaulted by a screaming mass of humanity that never listened to the music they came to play. They were, as Harrison would later claim, nothing but "performing fleas"—too distant to be seen clearly and incapable of being heard. They sometimes stopped in the middle of a song without the crowd ever noticing. On that first night they were amused by the hysteria they created, but how could they feel amused when the absurdity reached the fifth, the tenth, the twentieth night? What was the point of performing in such circumstances? They showed up, the crowd went into paroxysms of joy, they climbed back into their armored car and headed for the airport to be ready for the same experience in another city the following day. Where was the satisfaction? The joy for them was creating music, but they could do so only in stolen moments. They spent most of their time offering themselves up in sacrifice to the insatiable beast. When Brian Epstein broached the idea of a follow-up tour of Britain, they unanimously vetoed it. He kept pleading, and ultimately they agreed to a short tour in December—just nine concerts—but it would be the last British tour they would ever undertake.[4]

After returning from the States in 1965, they spent almost six weeks decompressing. When they were drawn back into the fray by the need to come up with a new album for the holidays, they came back recharged. They had been at the top of their profession for two years, and they were older, more mature, and more sophisticated musically. Their next creation, *Rubber Soul*, marked a significant artistic leap forward. Harrison contributed "Think for Yourself" and "If I Needed Someone" for the album. McCartney came up with such strong compositions as "Drive My Car" and "I'm Looking through You." John Lennon was the most inspired of all, producing several distinctive, memorable, highly personal songs—"In My Life," "Nowhere Man," "The Word," and "Norwegian Wood."[5]

Lennon, who was mired in a spiritual crisis, poured himself into his music. He and George, at the pinnacle of their hard-won worldly success, had come to question and devalue its fruits. In their disillusionment they began reading spiritually oriented books such as the Bhagavad Gita, the Bible, and *The Tibetan Book of the Dead*. Lennon's despair reached such depths that one night he got down on his knees in a locked bathroom and appealed to God for direction in his life.[6]

In the midst of the sessions for *Rubber Soul*, on October 26, 1965, the Beatles enjoyed a crowning moment of sorts. They were summoned to

Buckingham Palace so that Queen Elizabeth II could personally bestow medals recognizing them as Members of the British Empire—an honor usually reserved for a lifetime of service to the realm. Their elevation rankled many earlier MBE recipients, and a few were so outraged that they returned their medals in protest.

In fact, the criticism had some validity. The Beatles were not the lovable "mop tops" the world had seen in *A Hard Day's Night* and *Help!* Nor were they the well-scrubbed "lads next door" portrayed by their publicity machine. They were the products of a hardscrabble upbringing in Liverpool and not far removed from the decadent world of St. Pauli, with its boozing, pill popping, and sharing of groupies and hookers. The devil-may-care attitude of Hamburg days almost broke through to the public a few months later. Fed up with having to project a cuddly image, they proposed as a cover for the *Yesterday and Today* album a photo of themselves in butcher's aprons strewn with cuts of meat and decapitated dolls. At the last moment production was stopped, and all but a few of the ghoulish covers were papered over with a substituted photo of the band as the clean-cut pop stars their management wanted the public to idolize.

Nor were the Beatles upholders of the kind of beliefs the queen—as head of the Church of England—wanted to instill in her subjects. John and Ringo had been christened as Anglicans, Paul and George as Catholics, but all had drifted far from those moorings. In an interview almost exactly a year before their meeting with the queen, Paul stated matter-of-factly: "None of us believe in God."[7]

Harrison found no satisfaction in Catholicism. He had stopped going to Mass before his confirmation—rationalizing that he would confirm his faith later on his own—and over time he developed a jaundiced view of the Holy Church. The local priest would come through the neighborhood once a week, sending a child ahead to give notice by knocking on doors, George recalled. "And we'd all go, 'Oh shit!' and run like hell up the stairs and hide. My mother would have to open the door and he'd say, 'Ah, hello Mrs Harrison, it's nice to see you again. . . .' She'd stuff two half-crowns in his sweaty little hand and off he'd go to build another church or pub."[8]

Harrison also had a jaundiced view of church attendance. He once expressed his opinion that 99 percent of churchgoers showed up for services on Sunday morning only because they believed that if they didn't, God would hold it against them. He was especially disturbed that so many people appeared more preoccupied with the trappings of religion than with its spiritual value. To him, too many people felt that simply attending church on Sunday to be counted among the faithful was sufficient to earn God's forgiveness, and afterward they could return to what they were doing before. He felt that religion was "all screwed up" because it seemed to have no heart—that it ought to be about how people treated other people and what they gave to others, not what they received as believers.[9]

John, Paul, George, and Ringo were emblematic of the change occurring in Britain in the early 1960s. An increasing number of British were growing secularized and losing their religion. The Beatles' music offered vivacity and excitement, and the good feelings it stirred in people could not be matched by any religious figure. When John Lennon offered his opinion in the fateful interview with the London *Evening Standard* on March 4, 1966, he felt that he was merely stating the obvious: "Christianity will go. It will vanish and shrink. I needn't argue with that; I'm right and I will be proved right. We're more popular than Jesus now; I don't know which will go first—rock 'n' roll or Christianity."[10]

His remarks drew little response in Britain. For one thing, they were simply an aside in an article focused on Lennon's everyday life in the suburbs. In the United States, however, his comments were incendiary. The publisher of a magazine titled *Datebook*, trying to generate controversy to build circulation, made Lennon's provocative words the headline of the interview and sent advance copies of the issue to two flamboyant disc jockeys in Birmingham, Alabama. As he hoped, the DJs used it to stir up their deeply religious listeners. Within days, millions of churchgoing Americans considered the Beatles only one rung below the Antichrist in the hierarchy of demonic forces. Pastors railed against them in their sermons. Dozens of radio stations refused to play their records. Bonfires were started across the South to do away with their records and memorabilia.

The controversy could not have come at a worse time. The band was undertaking a world tour culminating in a series of open-air events in the United States. Instead of the fawning receptions to which they were accustomed, the Beatles now started to receive death threats. Brian Epstein considered whether to cancel the American leg of the tour.

Lennon felt no remorse over speaking his mind, especially since he was confident that his assertions were true. As a matter of principle, he didn't want to bow to public opinion. But this was not simply a matter of him alone. George and the others were being penalized and threatened because of something he had said. He ultimately agreed to address the controversy when the band arrived in Chicago to kick off the US tour. He tried first to explain to reporters the context of his comment, but he began to ramble and provoked more questions. Finally, he said, "I apologize if that will make you happy. I still don't know quite what I've done. I've tried to tell you what I did do but if you want me to apologize, if that will make you happy, then OK, I'm sorry."[11]

The tour went ahead—eighteen performances in seventeen days. In Washington, DC, the Ku Klux Klan picketed the show. In Memphis, an anonymous caller vowed to assassinate one or all of the Beatles during their concerts. (Their hearts leaped that evening when a firecracker exploded onstage.) In Los Angeles, the armored car in which they were leaving Dodger Stadium was overrun by scores of screaming teenagers and had to turn back. When they took refuge in offices below the grandstand, the crowd tried to break down the doors with battering rams. There was no way to know if they were simply enthusiastic fans or religious fanatics out for blood. They began to pelt the police with bottles, and the police responded with their nightsticks. Dozens were injured. The Beatles finally escaped through an exit at the opposite end of the field.[12]

Harrison found the venomous attacks on the band profoundly disturbing. "They used us as an excuse to go mad, the world did—and then they blamed it on us." He was especially put off by those who tried to portray their hostility and intolerance as carrying out the will of God. Though he no longer considered himself Catholic, or even a Christian, he had come to feel deeply religious himself. He characterized such acts as the burning of records as "trivialities," and as a believer in an afterlife he wondered how the self-righteous perpetrators would feel when they died and discovered how wrongheaded their behavior had been.[13]

After the final concert on the harrowing tour, at Candlestick Park in San Francisco, Harrison and Lennon felt immense relief. When he took a seat on the aircraft that night, George let it be known to all who were listening: "That's it, then. I'm not a Beatle anymore." For the whole tour he had been striving to convince John to join him in ending the madness. Lennon now agreed, sharing Harrison's unease about flying and being fed up with the narrow escapes and pointlessness of concerts in which no one cared what they played or if they played at all. McCartney still argued that they should keep the option open—that they couldn't be true entertainers without a live audience from time to time. But with Lennon siding with Harrison against the idea, Paul and Ringo could do nothing. From that day forward, the band would make their music in the studio. With the exception of the rooftop "concert" captured in the film *Let It Be*, the Beatles as a group would never again perform in public.[14]

Millions of people around the world continued to look at him with envy, but Harrison ceased to be satisfied with the life of a Beatle. He might have hungered at one time for fortune, fame, and life at the top, but now they no longer held any allure for him. "It was good fun for a while, but it certainly wasn't the answer to what life is all about."[15]

Finding that answer was to become his foremost goal.

Suggested Listening

"Love You To"

Part Two

The Making of a Mystic

4
Enlightenment

Wh—hen enlightenment did come for George Harrison, its arrival was facilitated by a substance known to scientists as lysergic acid diethylamide.

LSD was synthesized in 1938 by a Swiss chemist, Albert Hofmann, during experiments with compounds related to a fungus found on rye and other grasses. Accidentally exposed in 1943, he had out-of-body experiences and visual illusions provoked by sounds. Intrigued, he summoned the nerve to experiment with the substance deliberately. After the war, other researchers started exploring LSD's therapeutic potential, and in the 1950s the US military began studying it for military applications, such as a "truth drug" for interrogations. Aldous Huxley, the great British writer and explorer of consciousness, learned of its existence and sampled it in 1955. One of his correspondents was Dr. Humphrey Osmond, a psychiatrist working in Canada, who advocated doctors' taking LSD in order to understand their schizophrenic patients. Huxley proposed that LSD and other such substances be called *phanerothymes.* Osmond coined his own term, *psychedelics*—Greek for "showing the soul" or "showing the mind." In the early 1960s, Harvard researchers Timothy Leary, Ralph Metzner, and Richard Alpert conducted studies in which LSD was used for transcending awareness of identity and space-time dimensions.[1]

Harrison first tried LSD in early April 1965. John Riley, a thirty-four-year-old cosmetic dentist trained at Northwestern University Dental

School in Illinois, had returned to London to become a favorite of actors, models, and singers. He befriended the Beatles as patients and because of his affable personality was invited to visit the group in the Bahamas while they were filming *Help!* After their return to London for further filming, Riley invited George and John to come to dinner at his apartment at Strathearn Place, just north of Hyde Park. LSD had not yet been banned in Britain, and a friend of Riley's knew a chemist who manufactured the substance. The friend purchased some and had it delivered to Riley's home. At the time, Riley had no real inkling of the drug's potency. He and his girlfriend, Cyndy Bury, his hostess for that memorable evening, had no expectations of exploring new levels of consciousness or widening the Beatles' horizons. They merely saw LSD as the hip new thing to try.

When George and Pattie Boyd and John and Cynthia Lennon arrived at Riley's flat, Cynthia noticed something curious, although she had no clue to its looming importance: along the mantelpiece in the living room, arranged in a neat line, were four cubes of sugar. Riley probably expected that one of his guests would comment on the oddity, but none did, and following some conversation they moved into the dining room. After the meal they returned. George and John had planned to continue to the Pickwick Club to see their friend from Hamburg days, Klaus Voormann, perform with two other musicians, and George said, "Let's go." Cyndy Bury dissuaded them. She said that they hadn't had their coffee yet, and it was delicious. They sat back down. Riley conspicuously, but without explanation, dropped one sugar cube into each of their cups. After they drank their coffees, John Lennon insisted, "We *must* go now. These friends of ours are going to be on soon." But Riley unexpectedly said, "You can't leave." Lennon asked, "What are you talking about?" Riley answered, "You've just had LSD." When Lennon, who had read about the substance, understood, he was furious. None of the other three had heard of it.

They watched, alarmed, as colors began to grow in intensity and furniture seemed to shrink and elongate. Cynthia recalled, "It was as if we suddenly found ourselves in the middle of a horror film. The room seemed to get bigger and bigger. Our host seemed to change into a demon. We were all terrified." They collectively determined to get out of the room and dashed for the door without caring if their hasty exit appeared rude. In fact, their host and hostess took on the appearance of monsters trying to trap them.

Riley tried to persuade them to stay, growing increasingly desperate. Two of the world's most famous and beloved celebrities were dashing out into the streets of London with their brains scrambled, completely unprepared for what was about to happen to them, and he was responsible. His attempts to stop them were misinterpreted as interest in an orgy. They proceeded out to the street and hurried to the orange Mini Cooper George had given Pattie for her birthday. Riley offered to drive them so they could leave the car parked where it was, but feeling panic the four piled into the little Cooper, George behind the wheel. He drove them to the Pickwick, the tiny automobile seeming to grow smaller and smaller on the way. At the club they felt the full force of the LSD and found they couldn't deal with the distorted perceptions. They decided to go on to the Ad Lib Club, which was more familiar to them and was within walking distance. When they rode the elevator up to the club, a red light on the control panel led them to conclude that the building was on fire. As the doors opened to the fourth floor they were all screaming. Fortunately, Ringo Starr happened to be there, along with Mick Jagger and Marianne Faithfull, and John informed them what had happened.

Except for Cynthia, they calmed down somewhat. Pattie felt better and even turned playful. Although everything still struck John as terrifying, he found himself better able to cope—although he still could not think straight. When an admirer approached and asked to sit next to him, he gave him permission, but with the proviso that the man not speak to him. Cynthia spent the entire trip in a nightmarish dread that the substance had damaged her brain and the distorted perceptions would never go away.[2]

George found his terror transforming into awe. His perceptions broke free from the channels of nerve impulses carrying information from his surroundings to his brain—channels built up over a lifetime, channels that muffled input not important to survival. The floodgates opened. He was bombarded by a torrent of information from every direction and his five senses struggled to absorb it. Which of us has not been distracted by a noise or a glare or a scent we were not previously aware of, and afterward found it a challenge to resume our concentration? Which of us has not been enchanted by some texture or color we failed to appreciate at first? Now, imagine that fine-tuning of the senses multiplied by a thousand.

George perceived the world through the eyes of a mystic. The array of discrete objects around him—furniture, walls, buildings, trees, cars, animals, other people—blended into one continuous, teeming ocean of molecules, an ocean of energy that included even the transparent air that appeared to separate those objects. ("I could see the sap running through the trees and everything and I just knew there was such a thing as God. I suddenly felt happy that we were all connected to that energy. . . . The energy within me and the energy within you is all the same . . . and I could see the space between us was buzzing too!")[3] Further, the teeming ocean of molecules extended to include everything in the city, everything in the country, everything on the planet, everything, in fact, all the way to infinity. Each object, although it gave the illusion of being singular and definite, was in reality just a coalescence of atoms—a temporary coalescence. The atoms in any object—a plant, for example—do not cease to exist when it dies or is thrown on a trash heap. In time the atoms in any object dissociate, disperse, and are reconfigured in some new form. They are constantly in motion and constantly becoming. And if atoms from one object transform into other objects, in an endless process, then there is no real distinction between objects, only a ceaseless flux of forms within one unimaginably huge matrix that we label the universe. *Everything* is interrelated.

After the initial disorientation and fear of losing his sanity, George found his mood transformed in a positive direction. At the Ad Lib Club he became filled with a light that never truly left him for the rest of his life. He felt profound love for everyone in the room, everyone everywhere, and in fact, everything in the world. He saw existence as perfect and had an almost irresistible urge to tell all of the strangers in the club how much he loved them.[4]

The experience marked an epochal change for Harrison, searing into his brain a new understanding of the universe and his place in it. "Up until LSD, I never realized that there was anything beyond this state of consciousness. . . . The first time I took it, it just blew everything away. I had such an overwhelming feeling of well-being, that there was a God, and I could see him in every blade of grass. It was like gaining hundreds of years of experience within twelve hours. It changed me, and there was no way back to what I was before."[5]

The man most associated with LSD, Timothy Leary, once described how awe-inspiring the experience can be in a 1966 *Playboy* interview:

> What happens to everyone is the experience of incredible acceleration and intensification of all senses and of all mental processes—which can be very confusing if you're not prepared for it. Around a thousand million signals fire off in your brain every second . . . ; you find yourself tuned in on thousands of these messages that ordinarily you don't register consciously. . . . Some people are freaked by this niagara of sensory input. Instead of having just one or two or three things happening in tidy sequence, you're suddenly flooded by hundreds of lights and colors and sensations and images, and you can get quite lost.
>
> You sense a strange, powerful force beginning to unloose and radiate through your body. . . . It's as though for all of your normal waking life you have been caught in a still photograph, in an awkward, stereotyped posture; suddenly the show comes alive, balloons

out to several dimensions and becomes irradiated with color and energy. . . .

. . . Take the sense of sight. LSD vision is to normal vision as normal vision is to the picture on a badly tuned television set. Under LSD, it's as though you have microscopes up to your eyes, in which you see jewellike, radiant details of anything your eye falls upon. . . .

. . . Ordinarily we hear just isolated sounds: the rings of a telephone, the sound of somebody's words. But when you turn on with LSD . . . you hear one note of a Bach sonata, and it hangs there, glittering, pulsating, for an endless length of time, while you slowly orbit around it. Then, hundreds of years later, comes the second note of the sonata, and again, for hundreds of years, you slowly drift around the two notes, observing the harmony and the discords, and reflecting on the history of music. . . .

. . . The senses begin to overlap and merge. You not only hear but *see* the music emerging from the speaker system—like dancing particles. . . . You actually *see* the sound, in multicolored patterns, while you're hearing it. At the same time, you *are* the sound, you are the note, you are the string of the violin or the piano.[6]

Harrison recalled of his experience: "It was devastating because it cut right through the physical body, the mind, the ego. It's shattering because it's as though someone suddenly wipes away all you were taught or brought up to believe as a child and says: 'That's not it.' You've gone so far, your thoughts have become so lofty and there's no way of getting back." He later summarized his impressions: "It was like I had never tasted, smelled or heard anything before. . . . From that moment on, I wanted to have that depth and clarity of perception all the time."[7]

Harrison's life-altering revelation by means of a chemical has some fascinating parallels. In *The Road to Eleusis*, Albert Hofmann, the Swiss chemist who first synthesized LSD, and his coauthors R. Gordon Wasson and Carl A. P. Ruck, found notable similarities between the LSD experience, hallucinogenic cults of Mexico, and the ancient Greek initiation rites known as the Eleusinian Mysteries.

Wasson was an expert in ethnomycology, the study of the role of mushrooms in the history of humankind. In 1955 he took part in a spiritual initiation—what he termed "a midnight agapé"—under the guidance of a Mexican shaman, a ritual never before shared with a nonindigenous person. He ingested "magic mushrooms" and spent hours experiencing vivid sensory and psychological impressions. His description of the event is reminiscent of Harrison's and Leary's comments about the LSD experience: "It permits you to see . . . vistas beyond the horizons of this life, to travel backwards and forwards in time, to enter other planes of experience." "This newness of everything . . . overwhelms you and melts you with its beauty." "All these things you see with an immediacy of vision that leads you to say to yourself, 'Now I am seeing for the first time, seeing direct, without the intervention of mortal eyes.'"

In the aftermath of the experience, Wasson took an intuitive leap that some similar experience might lie behind the secret that has perplexed historians for centuries—the Eleusinian Mysteries. For almost two thousand years, uninitiated seekers who qualified prepared themselves each September and undertook a pilgrimage to Eleusis. There they witnessed the revelation of a great and profound truth—a truth considered so holy that it was never to be divulged, on pain of death. Clues from ancient texts suggest that the mystery involved secrets about the myth of Persephone's descent into the underworld and her resurrection each year, which was seen as an encapsulation of the story of humankind's rise from barbarism to civilization by means of the cultivation of crops. However, such a revelation hardly seems worth concealing under the threat of death. Other clues are more suggestive: apparently, something happened during the rites that filled the participants with soul-gripping religious awe. Whatever the experience was, it so profoundly influenced the initiates that they spoke of it in reverential tones for the remainder of their lives.

What Wasson found especially fascinating was that a key part of the initiation process involved imbibing a drink known as *kykeon*. He mulled over the subject for two decades and in 1975 approached his friend and colleague Hofmann with the question: Could the ancient Greeks have stumbled onto some primitive way to do what Hofmann had done—derive a psychoactive agent from ergot fungus on the rye growing in the vicinity of Eleusis? If so, that development could have led to its use in a religious context and ultimately resulted in the formalized ritual found at Eleusis. It could well be that every September the neophytes—with brains supercharged by *kykeon*—had been guided through an ancient sound-and-light show intended to shake them to the core and weld them together in a spiritual brotherhood.

After reflection and further study, Hofmann came to agree with Wasson. So did Carl Ruck, a scholar with specialized knowledge of ancient Greece and the Eleusinian Mysteries. Other experts challenged the conclusion the three reached in the first edition of *The Road to Eleusis*, but after reexamining the facts, chemist Peter Webster underscored how easily the Greeks could have accomplished what Wasson suspected. According to Webster, inquisitive Greeks could have concocted a psychoactive beverage simply by using wood ash slurry as a base and employing trial-and-error methodology.

And the parallels did not end with Mexico and Greece. Ruck, citing a paper by C. Watkins, points out similarities between *kykeon* and the mysterious Indian drink *soma*—not only in its ingredients and preparation, but also in elements of the ritual in which it was used. To assume that across the ancient world many people were initiated into mysticism by means of psychoactive substances found in nature does not seem far-fetched.[8]

In the grips of their own modern *involuntary* initiation, George, John, Pattie, and Cynthia finally decided to take refuge in George's house in Esher. He drove the Mini so slowly during the return trip that the nineteen-mile drive took an hour, although they perceived the buildings as whipping past. They arrived about dawn and locked the gate so no one would happen in and find them out of their minds. All of them stumbled into bed except for Lennon, whose imagination was on fire. He felt a compulsion to draw, and in one of his sketches four heads blended and announced: "We all agree with you." He remained awake for hours after the others, convinced that the house was a submarine and that he had to stay at the helm and steer.[9]

Two decades later, in 1987 Harrison recalled, "[LSD] just opened the door and I experienced really good things. I mean, I never doubted God after that. Before, I was a cynic. I didn't even say the word God; I thought 'bullshit to all that stuff.' But after that, I knew. It was not even a question of 'Is there possibly a God?'—I knew absolutely. It's just that big light that goes off in your head."[10]

Ostensibly agreeing, John Lennon later said, "God isn't in a pill, but LSD explained the mystery of life. It was a religious experience."[11]

Because he shared exactly the same introduction to LSD as Harrison—and presumably a similar experience—a dissection of their comments is instructive. Harrison "never doubted God after that" and claimed, "I knew absolutely." But Lennon's "religious experience" left room for doubt: "God isn't in a pill." By the end of that very same year, John would suffer a spiritual crisis. At one point he got down on his knees in a locked bathroom to beg God for direction. A year later, when he found a source and began to take LSD regularly, he was inspired to write "Rain" and "Tomorrow Never Knows." A year after that he came up with "A Day in the Life," "All You Need Is Love," and "Lucy in the Sky with Diamonds." Yet in 1970, while George was at work on his hymn "My Sweet Lord," Lennon wrote "God," in which he dispassionately summarized the deity as "a concept by which we measure our pain."

LSD *did* transform John's life. Cynthia Lennon watched her husband become more tolerant and loving, saying it was "like living with someone who had just discovered religion." Yet Lennon came to view God in a demystified, almost secular way. When asked directly, "Do you believe in God?" he responded, "Yes. I believe that God is like a powerhouse, like where you keep electricity, like a power station. And that he's a supreme power, and that he's neither good nor bad, left, right, black or white. He just is. And we tap that source of power and make of it what we will. Just as electricity can kill people in a chair, or you can light the room with it."[12]

Harrison, on the other hand, convinced that he had been touched personally by God, would become a devotee of Krishna. "If there's a God, I want to see Him. It's pointless to believe in something without proof, and Krishna Consciousness and meditation are methods where you can actually obtain GOD perception. You can actually see God, and hear Him, play with Him."[13]

George tried LSD again in August 1965, when the Beatles stopped in Los Angeles. Though better prepared this time because he knew what to expect, he was still blown away by its power. Peter Fonda attended the same party. When George expressed anxiety that he might be dying, Fonda tried to reassure him that he was all right—because Fonda knew what it was like to be dead. He had accidentally shot himself when he was a child and was briefly considered dead. John Lennon took part in the conversation and used phrases from it in his song "She Said, She Said."[14]

In the winter of 1966, Harrison found a steady source of LSD and began to trip out on it regularly. His creativity surged. He contributed three songs to the *Revolver* album—"Taxman," "I Want to Tell You," and "Love You To." The last was notable for its emphasis on the sitar and the fact that no other Beatle performed on the track.

From that winter of 1966, when he found a dependable supply, Harrison experimented with LSD for about eighteen months. Then, in August 1967, he had an eye-opening experience. While visiting California, he and Pattie chartered a plane to fly north to see firsthand "The Summer of Love" in San Francisco, which had become the undisputed capital of hippiedom. The gravitational center of the world's free spirits was the neighborhood that spread out from the intersection of two streets—Haight and Ashbury. There, "flower power" ruled. There, the sweet scent of incense mingled with the tangy aroma of ganja. There, head shops offered hookahs, roach clips, spoons, rolling papers, lava lamps, and black lights with psychedelic posters of Hendrix, the Byrds, and Jefferson Airplane. Mellow people wearing flowers in their hair and love beads around their necks hugged each other, shared possessions, and offered each other tokes and tabs and sugar cubes. Life was gentle and perfect.

Or so George imagined. For his visit to Shangri-la he dressed in paisley trousers and wore sunglasses with lenses shaped like hearts. He and Pattie and their friends took acid on the way to be prepared. Then a limousine dropped them off near the fabled intersection. As they strolled into a shop, voices were already calling out, "The Beatles are here!" A crowd formed, gawking. When Harrison returned to the street, they began to follow him in a mass. Directionless themselves, they treated him like the Messiah, the leader who had come down from the clouds to walk among them. ("Hey, man, want a joint, man?") They crowded near, following him so closely that he felt them stepping on his heels. ("Let me lay this peyote on you, man.") ("I got a book, man.") He and Pattie kept moving forward out of fear of being overwhelmed.

When they reached a park they tried sitting down in the grass. The entourage gathered in front of them as though forming an audience. These were not the Children of the Light he was expecting, but dropouts, panhandlers, street people. They were slovenly, strung out on every kind of drug. George winced as he noticed a guitar being passed above their heads in his direction. Unable to focus because of the LSD, he strummed a few chords, stood up, then handed the guitar back. Knowing they were disappointed, he began a retreat in the direction of the limo. "Sorry, man, we've got to go now." Some Hell's Angels approached him. To make conversation he told them to look him up if they ever came to London, little suspecting that they would follow up on his invitation. Then a man offered him some STP—a powerful, dangerous hallucinogen. When George rejected the offer, the man remarked to the others, "George Harrison turned me down." Suddenly there was an undercurrent of hostility. Harrison's group increased its pace. George recalled: "We just wanted to escape from this scene . . . which was like the manifestation of a Hieronymus Bosch painting getting bigger and bigger. Fish with heads, faces like vacuum cleaners coming out of shop doorways . . ." They reached the limousine and took refuge inside, but the crowd flowed around the big car and began to rock it, faces pressed to the windows. Finally the limo was able to pull away, leaving the tumult behind.[15]

After his Haight-Ashbury experience, George ceased to use LSD. He had seen where it could lead—disconnection, dissipation. "It certainly showed me what was really happening in the drug culture. It wasn't what I'd thought—spiritual awakenings and being artistic—it was like alcoholism, like any addiction." In an interview that fall he commented: "Although it's good in some respects, LSD isn't good because your mind isn't pure. . . . It's not good for your mind. It makes your mind rot after a while."[16]

When he returned to England, he told John Lennon about his experience and his decision not to use the substance anymore. Lennon took the point immediately. In fact, he was arriving at the same conclusion himself, having seen LSD's limitations and beginning to worry about the long-term—and possibly irreversible—effects on his brain. He, too, stopped using the drug.

Later on, George said: "You see the potential that it has and the good it can do but you also see that you don't really need it. I needed it the first time I had it. It was a good thing, but it showed me that LSD isn't really the answer to everything. It can help you go from A to B but when you get to B you can see C and you see that to get really high you have to do it straight. There are special ways of getting high without drugs—with yoga, meditation, and all those things."[17]

LSD had opened a door, but once Harrison passed through the door he found that true enlightenment lay in the wisdom of an ancient land.

5

Ravi and the Maharishi

From the moment in the Bahamas in February 1965 when Swami Vishnu-devananda gave him a book on yoga, George Harrison began to fall under the spell of India. Back in London for further filming, he heard an Indian musician play the sitar and was enchanted by its sound. That summer in Los Angeles he was introduced to the music of Ravi Shankar, and he conceived the idea of one day meeting the Bengali master. That fall he bought a sitar of his own and used it on one of John Lennon's songs. In early 1966 he wrote "Love You To" specifically to showcase the instrument. He began to attend recitals of the Asian Music Circle, which took place in the home of an Indian named Ayana Deva Angadi. Angadi not only knew Shankar, he promoted his concerts in London.[1]

In June 1966, Shankar came to London to perform at Albert Hall and Angadi invited Harrison to dinner in order to introduce them. Only vaguely aware of the Beatles and their wild success—he had not heard any of their songs—the sitar virtuoso was nevertheless impressed by Harrison. He wrote, in 1997, "I felt strongly that there was a beautiful soul in him, and recognised one quality which I always have valued enormously and which is considered the principal one in our culture—humility. Considering that he was so famous . . . he was nevertheless quite humble, with a childlike quality which he has retained to this day."[2]

Their personalities meshed, and Shankar agreed to come to Harrison's home and give him lessons. He insisted, however, that the sitar could never be mastered without devoting some time to its study in

India, to understand the culture that had given it birth. He used the analogy of an Indian wanting to master opera without speaking Italian or understanding Western culture or the Renaissance era.

Ravi visited George's home in Esher and showed him how to sit properly and how to cradle the bowl of the sitar against his left foot. He taught him some elementary scales and melodies. Harrison also learned that the instrument was not meant merely for entertainment. Ragas passed down from the ancient Vedas had a spiritual intent—the patterns of sounds had the capability to elevate consciousness. George was enraptured. "I felt I wanted to walk out of my home that day and take a one-way ticket to Calcutta. I would even have left Pattie behind in that moment."[3]

In July 1966, during a Beatles' stopover in New Delhi, Harrison finally purchased a high-quality sitar. In mid-September, two weeks after the group completed the final tour, George and Pattie flew to Bombay. There, under Shankar's personal tutelage, he began to learn the instrument. Taking the master's advice to heart, he also began extensive reading about Indian religion and culture. Ravi, who in his teenage years had met Paramahansa Yogananda, gave George a copy of *Autobiography of a Yogi*. In 1997, George wrote, "The moment I looked at that picture of Yogananda on the front of the book, his eyes went right through me . . . , and to this day I have been under the spell of Yogananda." He also studied *Raja Yoga* by Swami Vivekananda, as well as the time-honored *I Ching*.[4]

From these three books, it is easy to deduce where his interests lay. The first volume teemed with anecdotes about Indian holy men—their displays of telepathy, clairvoyance, telekinesis, levitation, existence without breathing, and other wonders. Yogananda died in Los Angeles in 1952, and the book includes a notarized statement by the mortuary director of Forest Lawn Memorial Park that when the yogi's casket was finally sealed with a bronze cover—twenty days after his death—his corpse displayed no sign of decay. *Raja Yoga* explained how yogic techniques could help one acquire the paranormal skills Yogananda mentioned. Swami Vivekananda was the earliest yogi to achieve fame in the West—widely recognized as the star of the World Parliament of Religions in Chicago in 1893. He wrote, "The Yogi teaches that the mind itself has a higher state of existence, beyond reason, a superconscious state, and when the mind gets to that higher state, then this knowledge, beyond reasoning, comes to man." The remarkable swami included a minicourse on how to reach the higher state, and he stressed that no assertion should be accepted without first proving it for oneself. His science-based approach impressed such disparate thinkers as Nikola Tesla, Mohandas Gandhi, and William James. The third book, the millennia-old *Book of Changes* from ancient China, revealed the hidden forces at work in the world by explaining the meaning of varying combinations of sixty-four tiles decorated with mysterious hexagrams.[5]

George and Pattie remained in India for five weeks, Harrison practicing the sitar daily and both receiving instruction in yoga. They also toured the ancient land with Shankar, visiting Srinagar, Jaipur, Jodhpur, Delhi, and Ravi's birthplace, the holy city of Benares. They saw the physical and cultural vestiges of the five-thousand-year-old civilization—temples, carvings, ruins, a maharajah, painted ascetics, centenarian holy men, elephants, peacocks, funeral pyres on the banks of the Ganges. The greatest spectacle of the tour was the Kumbh Mela festival, in which swarms of pilgrims—millions, in fact—converged on the city of Allahabad for purifying rites.

They also visited Vrindavan, according to tradition the village where Krishna himself had lived when he walked the earth. Ravi Shankar wrote of it: "Vrindavan is an astonishing place. Even today people there still talk of Krishna as if he is still a little boy in their neighborhood. It is said you can still hear him playing his flute in the city." Everywhere they walked, people chanted to the glory of Krishna. Harrison joined in with them and felt a natural high.[6]

"I think too many people here have the wrong idea about India," George observed after returning. "Everyone immediately associates India with poverty, suffering and starvation but there's much, much more than that. There's the spirit of the people, the beauty and goodness. The people there have a tremendous spiritual strength which I don't think is found elsewhere." The omnipresent spirituality in the ancient land impressed him deeply. He contrasted the deep religious feeling in India with the superficiality he seemed to find in Christianity in the West, in which people "turn it on Sunday morning" to go to church services. The Indians, on the other hand, appeared to integrate their religious feelings into everyday life—their thought, their actions, their conduct. They seemed to be spiritual every minute of their lives.[7]

He gave a clue to the direction in which he was moving spiritually, quoting from Swami Vivekananda's *Raja Yoga*: "They tried to bring me up as a Catholic, and for me it didn't deliver. But to read, 'Each soul is potentially divine. The goal is to manifest that divinity'—and here's how you do it!—was very important for me. That's the essence of yoga and Hindu philosophy."[8]

George and Pattie returned to England in late October, exhilarated by their experience. George kept up his daily yoga and practice on the sitar, and three months later discovered and became enthralled by a strange record album. An Indian holy man named Swami Prabhupada had come to the West to spread knowledge of a Hindu sect that worshiped Krishna. In the Hindu view of life, sound vibrations had mystical and beneficial properties, and chanting was an effective way to harness these properties and get in touch with God. Prabhupada went further. He asserted that Lord Krishna was embodied in the very pronunciation of his name. By chanting his name reverently, the devotee could commune with the deity. Voicing the *maha-mantra*—the phrase "Hare Krishna, Hare Krishna, Krishna, Krishna, Hare Hare, Hare Rama, Hare Rama, Rama, Rama, Hare Hare"—was a simple way to become one with God.

George had an affinity for Indian chanting from the first moment he heard it. He sensed the opening of some subconscious door—as though it brought back memories of a previous life. He played the record for John Lennon. The two were so enamored that they ordered a hundred copies to give away and began to chant regularly. On a vacation to Greece that summer, they chanted for hours while sailing the waters of the Aegean, accompanying themselves on ukulele banjos, enthralled, unable to stop.[9]

In early 1967 the Beatles began composing songs for their next album—*Sgt. Pepper's Lonely Hearts Club Band*. One night Harrison visited the home of Klaus Voormann, a German friend from Hamburg days who had relocated to London. With both high on marijuana, and George inspired by his growing passion for Indian philosophy, they fell into a discussion of the needless gulf between individuals and how it could be overcome by love. Tragically, George believed, most people never did grasp this truth, being distracted by the appearance of things and their egocentric views. From the Hindu perspective, they never woke up to the world's illusions until the time of their death—when their temporary visit to this world ended. In a break in their conversation, Harrison strolled into another room. He came upon a harmonium and idly began to tap keys. A melody and lyrics began to take shape: "We were talking about the love between us all / and the people who hide themselves behind a wall of illusion." Working out the words, George realized that he had the chance to do something that had never been done—infuse the Indian aesthetic into Western pop music. Creating the song became a labor of love, and when he was ready to record he invited a group of Indian musicians to support him. George Martin deftly integrated violins and cellos, but no other Beatle performed on the track.

"Within You without You" was one of the most original and distinctive songs the Beatles ever created, a gem in the album generally considered the pinnacle of their career. And only one Beatle could be given credit for it. Songwriter and performer Stephen Stills considered George Harrison's lyrics so profound that he had them carved in stone in his yard.[10]

When the time came to design the album cover for *Sgt. Pepper*, each Beatle was asked to name iconic figures to create the crowd scene.

While the others picked such celebrities as Johnny Weissmuller, Marlon Brando, Laurel and Hardy, Shirley Temple, and Edgar Allan Poe, George revealed his new predilection for Indian holy men. He chose Paramahansa Yogananda and the three predecessor gurus through whom the ancient wisdom had come down to him.[11]

Pattie, too, was inspired by the visit to India. In February 1967 she went to a seminar in London and was initiated into a group founded by yet another Indian holy man working to introduce Hindu wisdom to the West. This man's guru had taught him a quick and efficient way to enter a deep state of meditation. After his master's passing he felt it was his mission to spread this technique around the world as a way to bring peace and contentment to societies everywhere.

In August 1967 this spiritual leader, Maharishi Mahesh Yogi, came to London to speak prior to taking a group of his advanced initiates on retreat in Wales. George and the other Beatles, who through Pattie had discovered and begun to appreciate the Maharishi's meditation technique, made it a point to attend his lecture on the twenty-fourth at the Park Lane Hilton. (Only Ringo did not attend, his son Jason having been born just days before.) At George's urging, they had all read *Autobiography of a Yogi*, with its matter-of-fact anecdotes of supernatural feats, so it is easy to imagine the sort of holy man they expected to see.

What they encountered was a fifty-year-old man with long, straggly hair and a high-pitched voice who tended to punctuate his spiritual discourses with nervous giggling. That habit did not detract from his charisma, however, since his cheerfulness seemed to derive from some inner light. He also had a very appealing message. He had come to relieve the strife in the world by teaching a simple technique anyone could learn. While he might have spent years in self-renunciation, living in the Himalayas, that was not necessary for everyone else. Anyone could learn this technique without altering his or her current lifestyle. After a few sessions those who tried it would begin to be transformed. His thinking was that the more people who tried it, the more widely a wave of love and peace would spread across the planet.

All of the Beatles found the message attractive, but it hit the mark for Harrison and Lennon. Lennon had been battling his own demons ever since he reached the top to discover that success, and life in general, seemed meaningless. Harrison had been striving to understand the implications of his inner changes as a result of his LSD experience. Both now saw an answer within their grasp, and by following the Maharishi's agenda they thought they could achieve their own purposes. The Maharishi invited the Beatles up to his suite after the presentation. Seeing their interest, the holy man asked them to come along as guests on the retreat he was about to host in Bangor, Wales. The retreat was intended for personal instruction of his most advanced pupils, but the Beatles' publicity value won them a free pass. The only condition—they would have to give up drugs.

They decided as a group to drop everything and attend. The next day they caught the train to Bangor. Upon arrival, they settled into austere accommodations—a college dormitory—and on Saturday morning held a press conference in which they described their interest in the Maharishi's teachings and announced they had given up drugs.

The very next day the group were confronted with a development that tested their spirituality. News came that Brian Epstein had died during the night. The cause, at the time, was a mystery, although a drug overdose of some kind seemed likely. Reeling, they received an invitation from the Maharishi to join him in his quarters. They found him awaiting them in the midst of a roomful of flowers, serene and in the lotus position. He consoled them about Brian's passing by assuring them that all was well. Tears would not bring him back, but instead might keep his spirit earthbound. If they loved Brian and wished him well, they should not be sad but joyful. His spirit would then find peace and move on to the next world. The Maharishi's cheerfulness, as sunlight streamed through windows and struck a sea of multicolored flowers, transformed their dark mood.

They went back outside to face reporters, not morose but in good spirits. When Harrison was asked to comment, he said, "There is no such thing as death, only in the physical sense. We know he's okay now. He will return because he was striving for happiness and desired bliss so much." George would attend a memorial service at a synagogue in St. John's Wood, but to avoid creating a disruptive scene neither he nor any of the Beatles would go to the funeral in Liverpool. Instead he sent a single sunflower, which Epstein's business partner dropped into the open grave.[12]

Because of the tragedy, the Beatles decided to leave the retreat early. The Maharishi invited them to come to another retreat he was hosting in February 1968, which was to take place at his compound at Rishikesh, in India. Over the next few months, the Beatles kept up their meditation sessions and their contact with the guru, Paul and George flying to see him in Sweden to sort out some misunderstandings, and John and George joining him in Paris for a recital by Ravi Shankar.

Harrison and Lennon took part in a joint television interview with David Frost on September 30, 1967. Frost prodded Harrison about the Maharishi's claim that meditation led to increased energy. "The energy is latent within everybody," George said. "It's there anyway. . . . Meditation is a natural process of being able to contact that, so by doing it each day you contact that energy and give yourself a little more. Consequently, you're able to do whatever you normally do—just with a little more happiness maybe." Frost wanted to know if they had seen tangible results. George responded, "We've only been doing it a matter of six weeks maybe, but there is definite proof I've had that it's something that really works. But in actual fact it'll take a long time to arrive at the point where I'm able to hold that pure consciousness on this level or to bring that level of consciousness into this level of consciousness."[13]

Of all the Beatles, Harrison was the one most intent on integrating meditation into his life. In another interview, he was asked if it could become a substitute for religion for him. "It's not a substitute for religion," he said. "It *is* religion. The problem is that if you talk about it as a religion it puts people off because they have a concept of religion that has made religion unsuccessful."[14]

At the beginning of the year, Harrison returned to India. He had accepted an offer to produce the soundtrack for a film titled *Wonderwall*, a challenge that gave him the opportunity to work with Indian musicians at the EMI studios in Bombay. While there he also completed the backing tracks for "The Inner Light," another remarkable fusion of Asian culture and Western pop music. In the song he drew his lyrics from a translation of the Tao Te Ching, so the end result was ancient Chinese wisdom communicated by a modern European through music written for and performed by traditional Indian instruments. The record came out in March 1968, while the Beatles were on retreat in Rishikesh, and was the first song composed by Harrison to be released on a Beatles single, appearing on the reverse side of "Lady Madonna."[15]

In February 1968 a bevy of celebrities converged on a remote ashram in the foothills of the Himalayas. Known as the Academy of Meditation, the facility welcomed not only all four Beatles and their ladies, but also singer-songwriter Donovan Leitch, Mike Love of the Beach Boys, Mia Farrow and her sister Prudence and brother John, and flautist Paul Horn, along with dozens of other individuals who were intent on becoming trainers for the Maharishi's program. After the world's media gave up trying to spy on them through telephoto lenses, life at the ashram settled into a routine—waking up to the calls of peacocks, an open-air breakfast of porridge or cereal, morning meditation, vegetarian lunches and dinners followed by lectures by the guru at 3:30 and 8:30 p.m.—all against a serene backdrop of sunny days, chilly nights, pure air, and the soothing sound of flowing water from the nearby Ganges. In his lectures, the Maharishi explained what happened during meditation and what his listeners should be trying to achieve. He said some might undergo out-of-body experiences, and both George and Pattie felt they did. He also taught that there were seven levels of consciousness: waking, dreaming, deep sleep, pure or "transcendental" consciousness, cosmic consciousness, God consciousness, and Supreme Knowledge. Of these, he said, most people knew only the first three levels. The attendees were gaining experience in the fourth. The Maharishi said that his own guru,

Swami Brahmananda Saraswati, had attained the seventh and highest state. After a time the Maharishi suspended lectures to allow more time to meditate, and the more dedicated pupils began to undertake marathon sessions. George and John soon were spending eight or nine hours a day focused on their mantras. As committed as John was, he marveled at the intensity of George's pursuit of enlightenment. "The way George is going he will be flying on a magic carpet by the time he's forty."[16]

Ashram life was not for everyone. Ringo Starr left in the first two weeks. Not only did he find little satisfaction in the meditation, but his stomach would not accept most of the foods offered, and he and his wife Maureen were worried about their young children back in England. Paul McCartney and his girlfriend, Jane Asher, left after a month. He was concerned about the launch of Apple, the new enterprise the Beatles had formed to orchestrate their business interests.

George and John persisted. Several weeks into the retreat, John's friend Alex Mardas arrived. He was skeptical of the Maharishi and his influence over John, dismissing it as "black magic." Shortly after arriving, Mardas befriended an American nurse. He claimed that she informed him she had had sex with the supposedly celibate spiritual leader. He went to John with the information. John was skeptical at first, as was George. Cynthia Lennon believed that Mardas had concocted the accusation because he was jealous of the Maharishi's influence over John and wanted to sow discord. However, Lennon recalled that when Mia Farrow left the course early, there were allusions to inappropriate behavior by the guru. After an all-night discussion of the allegations, John and George went to confront the Maharishi. John informed him brusquely that they were leaving. When the guru asked why, Lennon said as a challenge, "You know why." The Maharishi had never demonstrated any of the supersensory abilities they all believed he possessed. Now was the time to show them if he did. The exchange went on, but no display was forthcoming—only, at last, a flash in the guru's eyes that Lennon interpreted as "I'll kill you, you bastard."[17]

Lennon and Harrison made the decision to leave. For George, the departure was especially bitter. He had enjoyed the escape from Beatlemania, and he found it profoundly satisfying to live a simple, meditative life. He knew the chief reason the others had come to Rishikesh—and in fact their interest in Indian mysticism in general—could be traced to his enthusiasm. But Ringo had shown the shallowness of his commitment, leaving the ashram in less than two weeks. Then Paul had placed greater priority on the new Apple enterprise than his spiritual life. Now even John, whose sincerity George thought matched his own, had cut short his commitment. Harrison felt isolated and alone in his spiritual quest.

When he reached Delhi, Lennon returned to London on the first flight available. George could not yet bring himself to abandon India. Instead, he took Pattie and her sister Jenny to Madras (modern Chennai) to spend time with Ravi Shankar and reflect.

6

Krishna

Achanged George Harrison returned to England. Apple employee Tony King, who knew him well and had been at Klaus Voormann's house the night Harrison began writing "Within You without You," saw the difference. "When I first met George in 1963, he was Mr Fun, Mr Stay Out All Night. Then all of a sudden, he found LSD and Indian religion and became very serious. Things went from rather jolly weekends, where we'd have steak and kidney pie and sit around giggling, to these rather serious weekends where everyone walked around blissed out and talked about the meaning of the universe."[1]

Pattie wrote that, even though she and George had come back from Rishikesh "renewed and refreshed," she was aware of a change in him. "He had become very intense in India: the experience seemed to have answered some of the nagging questions he had had about his life but it had taken some of the lightness out of his soul." Harrison continued to meditate and to chant, but now in an obsessive way. At times he seemed to find peace; at other times the sessions left him withdrawn and depressed. His moodiness came to affect her, to the point where she admitted feeling "almost suicidal."

During his visits to India, he had become fascinated by Krishna. Known as "the dark one," the god was easily distinguished by being shown with blue skin. He was often depicted in the company of a retinue of Gopis—lovely maidens who tended to his needs—charming them by playing his flute. Adding to the weight of Pattie's despair, George said openly that he felt a desire to become such a figure himself—a spiritual being surrounded by women.

Despite his spiritual hunger, the temptations of a rock star were still too much to resist. He had affairs with other women, and he became less guarded about them with Pattie. He invited a French girl who had just broken up with Eric Clapton to stay at their house. Pattie soon sensed that the relationship was more than just friendly. When she confronted George about it, he dismissed it as her imagination. Angry, she went to London to stay with friends. Six days passed before George called to tell her that the French girl had left.[2]

Meanwhile, the Beatles began work on their next album, which was titled *The Beatles* but came to be known as *The White Album*. Rishikesh had inspired them all. John, Paul, and George had come up with dozens of song ideas—even Ringo had one in mind. In the third week of May 1968, they went to work. They met first at Harrison's house to tape twenty-three demo recordings, then moved into the studio on May 30 and worked on the album intermittently through October 17. They had such an abundance of new material that, against the advice of George Martin, they decided to release a double album.

Besides taking far more time to record than any other Beatles album, *The Beatles* was notable for other reasons. George, accustomed to having two or at most three songs on any LP, contributed four. John, who had left Cynthia and become attached to Yoko Ono, broke an unwritten code by bringing her into the studio while they worked. Also, for the first time, the Beatles had a guest star on one of their records—Eric Clapton, whom George invited to play lead guitar for the classic "While My Guitar Gently Weeps."[3]

In the song's lyrics, Harrison's new perspective on the world comes through clearly. "I look at you all," he begins, addressing the countless millions who will hear his voice, and laments the tragedy of "the love there that's sleeping"—the latent love unexpressed by people who are distracted. He sees in the cluttered floor, which "needs sweeping," a symbol of their cluttered vision. The misdirected people he sees are "controlled," "bought and sold," unable to unfold the love inside. However, the world keeps turning. Surely we will learn from our mistakes—won't we? The ponderous cadence, the sorrowful voice, and the anguish of the guitar suggest that the answer is no. George, now feeling enlightened to the way things really are, sees all through the eyes of a melancholy prophet.

The isolation he felt was about to be partly alleviated by his encounter with like-minded souls. On a cold December day in 1968, a crowd waited outside the Apple building, hoping as always for a glimpse of one or more of the most famous entertainers in the world. In their midst stood a strange American in a high-necked Eastern-style robe with a head shaved except for a topknot known as a *shikha*. Yoko Ono arrived in a Rolls-Royce. As a doorman hurried to open her door she noticed the singular figure. "You must be one of George's," she said. "Come on in." The man followed her and was directed to a lounge where some fifty people waited for various reasons. The Beatles were involved in a meeting. When it broke up, the other three left the building, but George came and opened the lounge door. As soon as he spotted the man with the shaved head, he crossed the room and came straight up to him as though he knew him. "Hare Krishna," he said in greeting. "Where have you been? I've been waiting to meet you."

The surprised devotee of Krishna introduced himself as Syamasundara Das, a disciple of Swami Prabhupada. George recognized the latter as the man whose recording of Hindu chants had so captivated him two years before. He mentioned how he and John Lennon had started to chant after hearing the album and had spent hour after hour doing so while sailing among the Greek islands. While touring India with Ravi Shankar in late 1966, George had encountered Krishna devotees chanting in public and had happily joined in with them, and ever since he had been keen on meeting some of their Western counterparts.

Harrison said that what he was most interested in knowing was, out of all the deities in the Hindu pantheon, why *Krishna*? Why single him out for worship rather than Shiva, Brahma, Ganesh, or another god? Syamasundara replied that, according to the beliefs of his group, Krishna was God's original *personal* form, the source from which all the others came. He was the one who merited the most veneration. Intrigued, Harrison invited the devotee to come out to his home in Esher that weekend.

In the rich scent of sandalwood incense, the twenty-three-year-old Syamasundara told George and Pattie his story. He had been a Fulbright scholar turned professional skier, yet he felt spiritually hollow. Like the protagonist of Kerouac's *Dharma Bums* and *Desolation Angels*, he found himself keeping an eye on the forests of the Northwest from a watchtower, passing the time by reading about Eastern mysticism. Then, on a visit to Haight-Ashbury, he went to a branch of the International Society for Krishna Consciousness (ISKCON) and heard Swami Prabhupada lecturing about the Bhagavad Gita and the value of chanting. His life changed.

George, dealing with the anxiety-inducing relations between the Beatles and the crumbling of the Apple venture, was fascinated. He knew very well how meditation and chanting had sustained him during distressing times. He was also impressed by the devotee's buoyant spirit. He asked how the ISKCON members viewed death. Syamasundara explained that devotion to Krishna would be repaid by release from further births and a return to Krishna in his cosmic form. The essential requirement was to keep Lord Krishna in mind at all times, and reciting the Hare Krishna mantra made that a simple task.

Syamasundara said that his guru had sent him to England to organize a branch of the Krishna Consciousness movement. Indian residents had provided some aid, one example being the beaten-up pickup truck he had driven to Esher. The small group had set up a makeshift temple in London, which he invited George to visit.[4]

The London branch of the Krishna Consciousness movement consisted of five adults and one infant living in a chilly warehouse. The devotees had transformed one wall of the loft into an altar. Upon arriving, Harrison saw several photographs of men in robes nestled amid burning incense and lighted candles. Near them were two eight-inch brass statues with garlands draped around their necks, the female with a hand outstretched and the male holding a flute. The two represented Radha-Krishna, the dual nature of Krishna. George had seen much larger versions of them in India. There was also a small painting of Chaitanya Mahaprabhu, a sixteenth-century holy man who had originated the custom of chanting in the open air. The devotees said that in San Francisco they had decided one day to step outside their temple and chant outdoors. When Prabhupada found out, he encouraged them to continue, remarking that they must have been inspired by Lord Chaitanya.

George found in the group a fellowship he had been craving. When they pulled out some instruments, he played a harmonium and sang the Hare Krishna mantra with them. When they finished and bent down in homage to the altar, he joined them. Later they all ate Indian food together. Needing to leave for a recording session, he told them with great feeling, "I'm inspired here." He invited the group to come and visit him in Esher, and they would become regular visitors to his home.[5]

Harrison considered writing some songs in praise of Krishna and mentioned it to the group. They communicated this to Swami Prabhupada, who at once saw the value of linking up with the Beatles and encouraged them to release such songs. The group also suggested that the Beatles record the Hare Krishna mantra, knowing the effect it would have on youth. George instead recommended that the London devotees record the song themselves, and the Beatles would release it on their Apple label. This they did in the summer of 1969, with George playing organ and bass. The song reached the Top Twenty in Britain and received wide airplay around the world.

John Lennon shared George's fascination with the Krishna Consciousness group. When he recorded "Give Peace a Chance" in his Montreal bedroom in May 1969, Canadian devotees were in attendance. Upon moving into his seventy-two-acre Tittenhurst Park estate that summer, he invited the British chapter to live with him while their London temple was refurbished. When Swami Prabhupada came to England in September for his first visit, John invited him to stay in one of the guesthouses on his property.

George, John, and Yoko Ono engaged in a lengthy recorded discussion with Prabhupada at the recital hall at Tittenhurst, which came to be known as "the Temple." Among other topics, they talked about the search for a true guru, the power of mantras, various translations of the Bhagavad Gita, and disciplic succession.[6]

Prabhupada had been working on a book about Krishna, intended to serve as a reference text for the organization. He wanted to have it published, but lacked the funds. Knowing that Syamasundara had a good relationship with George and that it would be a minor outlay for someone with Harrison's wealth, he asked his disciple to make the request. Syamasundara resisted, afraid of jeopardizing his budding friendship. He explained to his guru that the main reason he had good relations with George was that he never asked for anything. He waited until George offered. But Prabhupada considered the book essential to what he was trying to achieve. He insisted. When Syamasundara asked how much was needed, Prabhupada responded that it would take nineteen thousand dollars. Stunned, Syamasundara tried again to emphasize that it was not a good idea. But his guru refused to accept his counsel. "Yes, yes it is. You'll see. Krishna will help you."

The next day, Syamasundara accompanied Harrison and a renowned sculptor, David Wynne, to select a slab of marble for the altar of the new ISKCON temple. George had offered to pay. The disciple fretted all day about his guru's request. How could he impose on Harrison when he was already being so generous? He kept waiting for a favorable moment to bring up the delicate subject. Late in the afternoon, as the sky grew overcast, they went to Wynne's house for dinner. Afterward the disciple realized that George would be leaving soon to return to Esher. The moment had come. He had no alternative but to make the request. He summoned his courage and told Harrison straightforwardly that Swami Prabhupada had instructed him to ask if George would donate money for a project. Exactly as he feared, Harrison's face "got increasingly grimmer and grimmer." As he described the book on Krishna and explained the purpose, "I could see this whole thing passing through his face thinking, Oh man, they are just another one of these groups. Here it comes."

He recalled that when he finished his appeal and paused, the room went quiet. Harrison "fixed me with this really belligerent stare."

Just then, with no warning, every light went out. "And BWAM! This bolt of lightning hit the house. . . . The whole house shook. The sound and the light were simultaneous."

For a long while they sat in tense silence, unable to see. When the lights came on again, Syamasundara glanced uneasily at Harrison.

He was surprised to see a big grin.

"Well," George asked, "how much is it then?" Syamasundara told him. George laughed. "Well, what can I do after that?"

He not only paid for publication of the book, he wrote an introductory note.[7]

7

The Hindu View

The version of Krishna worship that Swami Prabhupada introduced to the West served as the spine of George Harrison's spiritual beliefs for the rest of his life. Not that he felt limited to Prabhupada's teachings or that they dampened his interest in other streams of Hinduism and mysticism. He remained a spiritual explorer, willing to consider and experiment with different ideas.

In fact, the Krishna Consciousness movement, and the worship of Krishna in general, is only one strand of the highly complex and ever-evolving belief system that has come to be known as Hinduism.

Comparatively few people in the West have more than the haziest notion of what Hindus believe, even though the Hindu faith includes almost a billion followers and is the oldest of the world's major religions. Hinduism should be thought of not as a well-codified system of belief, but as a loose alliance of like-minded worshippers, with splinter groups subscribing to various doctrines and interpretations. Despite the diversity, all branches spring from one root—a root on whose authority they agree. This is the collection of ancient teachings known as the Vedas.

While it is generally accepted that most of the Vedas existed hundreds of years before the time of Jesus, no one has a clear idea of how much further back they can be traced. The origins disappear into the murky haze of prehistory. For many years, scholars widely believed that the teachings had arrived in the Indian subcontinent around 1500 BCE with the invasion of a people known as the Aryans. But excavations have shown that the region occupied by the native Indus civilization dried out and was abandoned four hundred years before the supposed invasion. Whatever the origins, it seems plausible that the earliest elements of the Vedas—the hymns of the Rig Veda—were created as early as the third millennium BCE. For thousands of years the teachings were transmitted orally; not until the Muslim invasion of India in the fifteen hundreds CE were they fully committed to writing.[1]

Each of the four Vedas (Rig Veda, Sama Veda, Yajur Veda, and Atharva Veda) is divided into four main stages: the Samhitas (hymns used in rituals, the earliest composed), the Brahmanas (descriptions of rituals), the Aranyakas ("forest treatises," practices developed by hermits who had renounced the world), and the Upanishads. The Upanishads also came to be known as the Vedanta ("end of the Vedas"), to which two later texts were added—the Brahma Sutra and the Bhagavad Gita. The Upanishads include the experiences and wisdom of ancient sages, or *rishis*; some two hundred Upanishads exist, but the first ten to twelve, the oldest, are the most revered. The Brahma Sutra is a collection of aphorisms and short commentaries intended to organize and interpret the Upanishads. The Bhagavad Gita (Song of God) is a treasured episode from the Mahabharata epic—a prodigious work of 1.8 million words, well over twice the length of the Bible. The Gita, as it is commonly known, recounts a conversation between the god Krishna and a prince named Arjuna on the battlefield with war about to commence—a conversation rich with moral and spiritual guidance. In his *Hindu View of Life*, Radhakrishnan says the Vedantic texts "form together the absolute standard for the Hindu religion." Though some sects have other holy texts that inspire or define their beliefs, "other scriptures sink into silence when the Vedanta appears."[2]

Hinduism is predisposed to be inclusive. At the foundation of the Hindu pantheon is the *Trimurti*—the three aspects of God: Brahma the Creator, Vishnu the Preserver, and Shiva the Destroyer. But there are many avatars of these gods and a host of lesser gods known as *devas* (if male) or *devis* (if female). All may be worshiped. Conflicting beliefs are not rejected, but instead tend to be assimilated or at least tolerated. The thinking is that God encompasses everyone and everything, and within the limits of their own experience and knowledge all men are on the pathway to discover this supreme deity. Therefore, each person should be free to worship in his or her own way. At one end of the spectrum that might mean totemism; at the other end highly advanced yogis revere a singular, abstract, infinite God. As Radhakrishnan writes, "Hinduism requires every man to think steadily on life's mystery until he reaches the highest revelation. While the lesser forms are tolerated in the interests of those who cannot suddenly transcend them, there is all through an insistence on the larger idea and the purer worship."[3]

Specific to Christianity, Radhakrishnan notes that belief in Jesus as the Son of God is not rejected outright. Nor is the worship of the harsh and vindictive Yahweh of the Pentateuch. Nor is the contradiction inherent in Jesus, the exemplar of love, declaring himself one and the same with this jealous God. To the Hindu, divinity is multifaceted. Think of your mother. She may console you when you have been hurt, scold you when you have done something wrong, and cook your favorite dish for dinner—all on the same day. She is not three different people; you are simply seeing her in three different roles. This broad and inclusive view makes it possible to accept that while one person may worship Krishna, other Hindus are devoted to Rama, Brahma, Vishnu, Ganesh, or some other manifestation of the divine.[4]

To the Hindu, the various views of God only *appear* to conflict or contradict one another. God is the universal and underlying spirit. The various ways we apprehend this spirit say more about us than they do about God. Descriptions given by humans are destined to fall short because they are striving to describe something beyond their powers to describe. The time-honored Indian parable about the group of blind men struggling to describe an elephant is very apt. The man touching the elephant's leg describes the elephant as like a pillar. The man who feels only the tusk says with equal certainty that it is like a plow. The one touching the animal's trunk assures the others that it is like a big snake. As for the blind man standing at the elephant's rear, well, he definitely encounters something beyond his powers to describe.

As George Harrison says in his introductory note to Swami Pradhupada's book *KRSNA*, "As GOD is unlimited, HE has many Names. Allah-Buddha-Jehova-Rama: All are KRSNA, all are ONE." On another occasion, Harrison points out, "All religions are branches of one big tree. It really doesn't matter what you call Him as long as you call."[5]

The Bhagavad Gita is probably the most beloved text of Vedantic literature, one reason being that it reveals its wisdom in a dramatic context. Arjuna, the leader of the Pandavas, is about to join battle with an enemy army led by his cousins. Suddenly paralyzed by indecision, Arjuna voices to his charioteer his doubts about the morality of killing his own kinsmen. Unbeknownst to Arjuna, his charioteer, Krishna, is in truth God assuming the form of a human. As the story unfolds Krishna advises Arjuna on a range of spiritual topics: among others, the difference between the material body and the eternal soul; the recognition of which kinds of actions can lead to liberation; the importance of finding a guru (*guru* is Sanskrit for "dispeller of darkness"); the value and reward of pure devotional service; and the way to reach *samadhi* (full knowledge of the supreme). Ultimately, in the eleventh chapter, Krishna divulges his Godhood. In a scene reminiscent of Yahweh revealing himself to Moses on Mount Sinai, he permits Arjuna a glimpse of his radiant, awesome glory.[6]

The short work of some seven hundred verses is often seen as an allegory about the "battlefield" of human life and has inspired hundreds of translations and commentaries, including ones by Mahatma Gandhi, the Maharishi Mahesh Yogi, and George's friend and spiritual guide Swami Prabhupada. Ralph Waldo Emerson discovered the Gita in 1831 and considered it a scripture on a par with the Gospels. His reading of the book had a major influence on his own philosophy of transcendentalism and inspired his friend and admirer Henry David

Thoreau. Thoreau took along a copy on his sojourn at Walden Pond, reading from it to start each day. "In the morning I bathe my intellect in the stupendous and cosmogonal philosophy of the Bhagavad Gita, since whose composition years of the gods have elapsed, and in comparison with which our modern world and its literature seem puny and trivial; and I doubt if that philosophy is not to be referred to a previous state of existence, so remote is its sublimity from our conceptions."[7]

Gandhi, who called Thoreau his guru, shared his reverence for the Gita. "I must confess to you that when doubt haunts me, when disappointments stare me in the face, and when I see not one ray of light on the horizon, I turn to the Bhagavad Gita, and find a verse to comfort me; and I immediately begin to smile in the midst of overwhelming sorrow."[8]

George Harrison started reading the Gita in 1965, when he began delving into Indian culture after becoming enchanted by sitar music and learning about Ravi Shankar. He came back to the book again and again, reading it to his mother for solace as she lay on her deathbed in 1970, informing Swami Prabhupada years later that he preferred to read one verse at a time over and over, even working the Gita's concepts into his songs. "That which I Have Lost," he once acknowledged, was "right out of the Bhagavad Gita."[9]

Part of the Gita's authority and appeal lies in its geographical and historical roots. The battle it mentions takes place on Kurukshetra Plain, a real geographical region some one hundred miles north of Delhi. To this day the area is considered hallowed ground to Indians and draws many tourists. And Krishna—like Buddha, Jesus, and Mohammed—appears to be a figure of history. Although there is dispute about his era—some place him as far back as the thirty-third century BCE—his birthplace is unequivocally placed in Mathura and he grew up in Vrindavan, cities that still exist, both now situated in the state of Uttar Pradesh. Remnant memories of Krishna's earthly visit and the stories that have grown around him as a person engender feelings of intense devotion among his followers. They visit such locales as the Seva Kunj grove in the same spirit Christians flock to the Garden of Gethsemane in Jerusalem and Buddhists to the Deer Park in Sarnath. George traveled to Vrindavan three times—on his first visit to India in late 1966, in the company of Ravi Shankar in February 1974, and with Krishna Consciousness friends in April 1996.

Though worshipped as the Supreme Godhead by ISKCON members, Krishna is considered by many other Hindus to be an incarnation of Vishnu. He tells Arjuna in the Bhagavad Gita (4:7–8), "Whenever and wherever there is a decline in religious practice, O descendant of Bharata, and a predominant rise of irreligion—at that time I descend Myself. To deliver the pious and to annihilate the miscreants, as well as to reestablish the principles of religion, I Myself appear, millennium after millennium." Among others, Rama and Gautama Buddha are also considered by many Hindus to be avatars of Vishnu.[10]

But those are from the distant past. Hindus believe that avatars continue to appear, and in fact one from modern times made an unlikely appearance, at George Harrison's request, on the most highly acclaimed creation in the history of rock and roll—*Sgt. Pepper's Lonely Hearts Club Band*.

In the autumn of 1861 a thirty-three-year-old Bengali accountant named Shyama Charan Lahiri was out walking among the foothills of the Himalayas. Unexpectedly, he heard someone call his name. He climbed a mountain in the direction of the voice and discovered there a young man with copper-colored hair who claimed to have been Lahiri's guru during a previous life. The man never identified himself, but in his presence Lahiri began to recall his past lives, and he came to understand that he was not speaking with some ordinary mortal. That night the mysterious friend materialized a golden palace on the mountain and initiated Lahiri into Kriya Yoga, an ancient and forgotten technique. He tasked Lahiri with reintroducing the knowledge into this new age.

Lahiri was not a mystic or a holy man but a man of business. Nevertheless, because of the personal power of the mystery man, he acquiesced and took instruction. He began to teach the yoga method and in time some of his pupils, too, met the imposing figure Lahiri came to refer to as Babaji. At various times Babaji was witnessed displaying supernatural abilities that included telepathy, levitation, physical appearance in more than one place at once, and resurrection of a dead man. He appeared to be about twenty-five years of age, but to one of Lahiri's disciples who summoned the nerve to ask him, Babaji replied that he was five hundred years old.[11]

In 1910 a follower of Lahiri, Sri Yukteswar Giri, took on a disciple named Mukunda Lal Ghosh. He soon gave the young man the religious name Yogananda and eventually added the title Paramahansa. In 1920 Yogananda experienced a vision urging him to travel to the West to spread the knowledge of Kriya Yoga. After teaching in the United States for a quarter of a century, Yogananda published his autobiography in 1946. In it, while chronicling his own life experiences, he recounted stories of both his guru and his guru's guru—Sri Yukteswar Giri and Lahiri Mahasaya—as well as their encounters with the mysterious Babaji. He even reported seeing Babaji once with his own eyes, just prior to his departure for America.[12]

Yogananda's *Autobiography of a Yogi* was one of George Harrison's most treasured books, one he read again and again. When the Beatles were compiling a list of onlookers for the iconic cover photograph of the *Sgt. Pepper* album, George's personal choices included Yogananda, Sri Yukteswar Giri, Lahiri Mahasaya, and the enigmatic Mahavatar Babaji. Accordingly, in the second row from the top of the group photo, directly above Paul McCartney and to the left of Stan Laurel in his bowler hat, is the artist's depiction of Babaji that Yogananda commissioned from his memory of meeting him in 1920.

From time to time, people still report encounters with the reclusive Babaji—both astral and in the flesh. Is the incarnation of a deity observing us right now from some sanctuary high in the Himalayas?

Suggested Listening

"Within You without You"
"The Inner Light"
"While My Guitar Gently Weeps"

Part Three

TAKING THE WORD TO THE WORLD

8

All Things Must Pass

O n April 10, 1970, Paul McCartney announced the release of his first solo album—and, incidentally, his departure from, and as a consequence the breakup of, the Beatles. He neglected to mention that John Lennon had brought the issue to a head six months earlier, when he informed his band mates privately that he "wanted a divorce."

In truth, the relationship had fractured long before that. The first hints of the disintegration came in 1966, when the band decided to stop touring. Boarding the plane after their last concert together, George Harrison remarked to the others that he was "not a Beatle anymore." Equally disenchanted was John Lennon: "I was always waiting for a reason to get out of the Beatles from the day I made *How I Won the War* in 1966. I just didn't have the guts to do it, you see."[1]

Momentum carried the group forward—all persuading themselves that the process of recording new songs in the studio would be satisfaction enough. But that only placed greater emphasis on the tensions that flared during recording sessions. John and Paul had started to tug in different directions creatively. George resented both of them for their lack of interest in his new songs. Paul attempted to pick up the managerial reins after Brian Epstein died, provoking a backlash from the other three. By the time they recorded *The Beatles* in the summer of 1968, they had lost any spirit of collaboration. The others served merely as a backing band for whoever had written a new song. Paul expected George to play his guitar exactly the way he heard it in his head when he composed his tunes, and when Ringo failed to deliver the drum work he wanted Paul would sometimes rerecord the drum track himself after Starr left for the day. Fed up and alienated, Ringo quit the group. He came back, but the strained relations continued.

They were captured on film months later in the documentary *Let It Be*. When filming began, Harrison had just spent time as Bob Dylan's houseguest in Woodstock, New York. Dylan had also invited members of his backup group, The Band, for the holidays. In that company, George rediscovered the simple joy of making music with talented people whose focus was not the credit or their own egos, but the music itself. Then he showed up for the *Let It Be* sessions and found himself embroiled once more in tense exchanges and tugs-of-war. To vent his frustration, on January 7, 1969, he sat down and wrote "I Me Mine." On one level the lyrics targeted Paul and John for being so fixated on their own interests. On another level they lamented the tendency of all of us to be egocentric. How many people could go through a day—or even one hour—without using the word "I"? Our ingrained self-centeredness "[flows] more freely than wine / All thru your life I me mine." What made the situation ironic (and tragic) from the Hindu point of view was that the ego is an illusion; we are all parts of a whole. Imagine one drop of water in an ocean fixating on its own agenda.

While he could draw back and look at their egoism (and his own) objectively, the daily struggles with Lennon and McCartney were still taxing. As the camera rolls, Paul at one point instructs George how to play his guitar: "I'm just saying you could try playing it like this." Struggling to remain civil, George replies, "I'll play whatever you want me to play, or I won't play at all if you don't want. Whatever it is that will please you, I'll do it." Shortly after that, he walked off the set, determined to leave the group. He stayed away for five days, coming back only after the others agreed to respect his concerns. For insurance he brought along Billy Preston, a pianist with an upbeat personality, having learned from his invitation to Eric Clapton earlier that John and Paul would be less overbearing in the presence of another professional.[2]

The end was coming. From their days as callow teenagers, through the mounting success of Hamburg and the Cavern, and on through their glory days as four of the most famous and envied men in the world, John, Paul, George, and Ringo had been bound together by a common background and a shared fate. They were all in it together, mates, flourishing and suffering as a group. They knew each other's strengths, faults, and eccentricities. But the one constant in life is change. Much as they might like to hold on to what was familiar, the four were evolving in different directions. The Beatles as a group were passing away.

Other pillars of Harrison's old life also were passing away. In June 1970 his mother, Louise, who had previously been diagnosed with cancer but had gone into remission, was readmitted to Liverpool Hospital. George traveled north to be with her. While she was there, his father, Harry, was brought to the same hospital for his ulcers. George divided his time between their rooms. Harry recovered and was able to leave the hospital. Louise did not.[3]

The month after McCartney made his announcement, Harrison began work on his own solo album. He had started to discuss the project as early as the previous fall. Having been limited to two or three songs on each new Beatles album by the more productive and more assertive partnership of Lennon and McCartney, he felt the need to put out an album of his own just to get rid of the backlog. Parsing them out at the current rate would require three or four years, and he was coming up with new songs all the time. To that end, he recorded and issued a triple album—unprecedented for a solo artist. He titled it after one of the strongest tracks, a name particularly apropos in view of the changes in his life: *All Things Must Pass*.

From the time LSD altered George Harrison's view of life and the universe and he fell under the spell of Indian religion and philosophy, he felt inspired to communicate the change he was undergoing. "Within You without You" was his first major attempt to spread the message. "The Inner Light" followed. When the Maharishi came into his life, "the Quiet Beatle" stepped into the limelight and got personally engaged, reaching out through the media to propagate the guru's message. When he came into contact with the Krishna Consciousness movement, he produced their recording of the Hare Krishna mantra and used his influence to make sure it received airplay. He also funded the publishing of Swami Prabhupada's book on Krishna and even wrote an introductory note.

Now that the time had come to define himself as a solo artist, he did not hesitate to emphasize his spirituality. "At that time, nobody was committed to that type of music in the pop world. There was, I felt, a real need for that. . . . So I thought, just do it. Nobody else is, and I'm sick of all these young people just boogeying around, wasting their lives." *All Things Must Pass* served as a declaration of his views to the world. I am a person of deep faith, he said musically; these songs are inspired by what I believe.[4]

Several songs on the album emphasized the influence of Indian religion. The majestic title track addressed the subject of transience: "Sunrise doesn't last all morning / A cloudburst doesn't last all day." There is no point, he was saying, in growing attached to the good times or the bad. Like a river, whatever we are experiencing is bound to flow past. We might as well accept the fact because there is nothing we can do about it. He also appears to offer a hint of his growing detachment from Pattie: "Seems my love is up / And has left you with no warning." *All* things must pass away.

The album's most popular tune—inspired by the Edwin Hawkins Singers' version of the hymn "Oh Happy Day"—was "My Sweet Lord." In it Harrison laid out his passion for God for all to see. His reverent tone resonated with millions of believers, many of whom failed to discern that Harrison's "sweet Lord" was Krishna. He deftly integrated into the song most of the Hare Krishna mantra, smoothing the way by first repeating the common word *Hallelujah* fourteen times. "I did the voices singing 'Hallelujah' first and then the change to 'Hare Krishna' so that people would be chanting the Maha Mantra—before they knew what was going on!" The song closed with a mantra honoring the Hindu holy trinity—Brahma, Vishnu, and Maheshwara (Shiva). "My Sweet Lord" rolled across the airwaves like a juggernaut, with commanding presence, much the way Dylan's "Like a Rolling Stone" had arrived in the mid-sixties. Elton John recalled his reaction the first time he heard the song: "I remember hearing 'My Sweet Lord' in a taxi somewhere, I can't remember what city, and I thought, 'Oh, my God,' and I got chills."[5]

In another strong track, "Awaiting on You All," George urged listeners to chant the names of God in order to cleanse their spiritual pollution and "be free." Turning to churches to find Jesus or temples to find God meant searching in the wrong places. Each person had but to look within. As Swami Vivekananda had written, the spark of the divine is within us all. Every person is therefore the child of God, and this spark can be fanned by chanting. In his autobiography, *I Me Mine*, Harrison explained that the song promotes *japa yoga*—the discipline of meditating on mantras while fingering through a strand of beads. Since each mantra "is mystical energy encased in a sound structure, and each mantra contains within its vibrations, a certain power," chanting has the ability to send spiritual energy through the body, leading to the enlightenment of the person chanting.[6]

"Art of Dying" offered a clear reference to reincarnation and the endless rebirths awaiting people "brought back by our desire to be." Those individuals who could not discover the truth for themselves were condemned to live through "a million years of crying." Harrison imparted his idea of the truth to them in his song, but he realized they would find it a difficult concept to accept. "Do you believe me?" he felt compelled to ask.[7]

All Things Must Pass proved to be the most successful album ever released by an ex-Beatle, remaining atop the US charts for seven weeks despite the stiff price for a three-LP boxed set. Critics were swept away by its scope—106 minutes of music, offering nineteen songs ranging from the profound to the whimsical, as well as jam sessions combining the talents of Ringo Starr, Eric Clapton, Dave Mason, Billy Preston, and others. *Rolling Stone's* Ben Gerson called it "the music of mountaintops and vast horizons" and summed up the epic album as "the *War and Peace* of rock 'n' roll."[8]

During his final years with the Beatles, Harrison had flowered as a creative force—able to penetrate the stream of Lennon-McCartney compositions with such gems as "Something," "Here Comes the Sun," and "While My Guitar Gently Weeps." However, other songs John and Paul dismissed would later become hits for George (for instance, "All Things Must Pass" and "Isn't It a Pity," both originating in 1966), and Harrison's muse continued to treat him well in 1970. The Beatles *could* have produced one more first-rank, single-LP album based solely on Harrison's work. As an exercise in imagination, visualize *All Things Must Pass* as the final Beatles release, anchored by "All Things Must Pass" and "Isn't It a Pity" (with Paul singing lead), "I Dig Love" and "Wah Wah" (John), "My Sweet Lord" and "Ballad of Sir Frankie Crisp (Let It Roll)" (George), "What Is Life" and "Art of Dying" (Ringo), and including such other strong tracks as "Awaiting on You All," "Behind that Locked Door," "I'd Have You Anytime," and "Beware of Darkness."

While working on *All Things Must Pass*, George lived in his newly purchased home—Friar Park—a twenty-five-bedroom, neo-Gothic house on thirty acres near Henley-on-Thames. He brought to it from his home in Esher many decorative elements he had acquired as a result of his fascination with Indian religion. But in Esher they had been displayed with a touch of whimsy. Hare Krishna devotees who visited him in Esher were both amused and put on edge when they saw, between images of Ganesh and Saraswati, the novelty-store print of cigar-smoking dogs at a poker table. The tone at Friar Park was more reverential. Harrison converted an octagonal room at the summit of the house into his private temple, covering the floor with Persian rugs and using it as a place to meditate. He also transformed a wine cellar into an echo chamber, the ideal venue for chanting. Shortly after he and Pattie moved in, he invited three Hare Krishna families to live in the huge house as service staff, the men to share in the gardening and the women to care for the house and cook. He thought this arrangement would benefit his fellow spiritual seekers, give him friends with whom to chant, and contribute to "good vibes" in the house.[9]

According to one of these devotees, Syamasundara Das, George's commitment to Hinduism was sincere and profound. "This wasn't just a casual sort of curious intellectual enquiry but rather a deep, deep longing for the truth." Harrison himself said, "Through Hinduism I feel a better person. I just get happier and happier."[10]

George struggled to pursue a spiritual life, but sometimes he couldn't resist the siren call of the world. His earnest efforts to perfect himself blew hot and cold, swings of mood he signified by changing the flag flying on top of the house's cupola—a banner featuring OM in Sanskrit when he felt in tune with his goals, a skull and crossbones when he did not. According to Chris O'Dell, an assistant who lived at Friar Park during this period, there seemed to be "three Georges in the house." On any given day, she and the other residents might encounter one or more of them. The first George was "great fun"—the man she had gotten to know while working at Apple. The second was "intense, sarcastic, and detached"—the curmudgeon vexed by his relations with the other Beatles or setbacks with the remodeling efforts. The third was "absorbed in otherworldly thoughts"—the spiritual seeker who seemed at peace but was not good company for housemates who preferred to talk, drink, and laugh.

A regular smoker of marijuana, which soothed him and kept his thoughts elevated, Harrison at times succumbed to the lure of cocaine. He would go for months without touching it, purifying himself through long hours of meditation. Then he would overindulge. During periods of withdrawal he would become a recluse in his own house. During cocaine binges he would turn abruptly social, but it was an artificial high that left Pattie still feeling out of touch with him. She could see that his passion for her had waned, and she attributed part of his coolness to the fact that she hadn't become pregnant over the years. The other three Beatles all had children by this time. After George and Pattie had fertility tests, George confided to close friends that he was the problem. But his confidants suspected he was saying so only out of gallantry. Their suspicions proved true when, in 1978, Harrison had a son by Olivia Arias.[11]

With no children to care for, Pattie had difficulty creating a satisfying life beyond her relationship with George. He had discouraged her modeling career early in their relationship, hating the public eye himself and preferring her not to draw more attention to them, and by mid-1967 she had all but stopped. She struggled to find other outlets for her time and energy, exploring meditation, yoga, knitting, art classes, even—briefly—flying lessons. For a time she found great satisfaction in cooking, but after the Krishna Consciousness members moved into Friar Park George discouraged even that because he came to prefer the Indian dishes they prepared.[12]

The attention he once lavished on Pattie he now devoted to the house and grounds, obsessively planning renovations and changes, or else he slipped off by himself to meditate. George's best friend, Eric Clapton, watched with conflicted feelings the deteriorating relationship with Pattie, knowing that all George had to do to reinvigorate his marriage was assure his wife that he still loved her. Clapton was conflicted because for years he had been secretly in love with Pattie while being best friends with George. Harrison had written "Here Comes the Sun" while strolling in Clapton's garden. Clapton had played lead guitar on Harrison's song "While My Guitar Gently Weeps." They had cowritten "Badge," a song for Eric's group, Cream. They frequently went to clubs and shows together in London. All the while, Clapton had hidden his passion for George's wife. Miserable, he finally communicated his feelings to her. Flattered, she met secretly with Eric on various occasions, though keeping the relationship platonic. Then, in late 1970, Clapton wrote "Layla" to express his inner torment. He played it for her on one of their trysts, and as she remarked, "I could resist no longer." Later that evening George arrived at a party after a long recording session and found his wife hand-in-hand with Clapton, away from the crowd, alone in the garden. When he demanded to know what was going on, Clapton admitted, "I have to tell you, man, that I'm in love with your wife." Angry, Harrison asked Pattie if she was coming home with him or was staying with Clapton. She returned home with him. Clapton, unable to reconcile himself to life without her, approached Pattie again while George was away. He told her that he couldn't stand the pain of not having her and said that if she wouldn't come with him he would cope by taking heroin. When she declined, he made good on his threat, sinking into heroin addiction for the next three years.[13]

George, meanwhile, got over his upset and maintained his friendship with Clapton. He also became less guarded about his attraction to other women. Of many affairs, the most scandalous was with Maureen Starkey, Ringo's wife. She began to show up at Friar Park regularly, saying she wanted to watch George recording in his studio. Pattie began to discover her still in the house the next morning. Once she caught George and Maureen in a locked bedroom while everyone was waiting for him in the studio. Furious, she climbed on the roof of the house and replaced the OM flag with the skull and crossbones.[14]

The situation was to grow even worse. Returning to Friar Park in December for a Christmas visit after moving to Los Angeles, Chris O'Dell discovered George and Maureen chatting intimately in one room while Pattie and guitarist Ron Wood flirted in another, each couple aware of but ignoring the other. The next morning Harrison confessed to Chris that he was in love with Maureen.

The following night, at Ringo's house, George and Ringo were sitting on one bench at a wooden table in the kitchen while Pattie and Chris sat across from them on the other side. While they chatted and listened to music from a jukebox in the next room, Maureen moved around the room playing hostess, bringing food and drinks. Chris noticed Maureen go to a nearby drawer and pull out a pack of Marlboro cigarettes. Marlboro was George's brand; Ringo and Maureen smoked Larks. Maureen brought the pack to George and smiled as she placed it near his hand.

For a moment there was a hush. Then George, echoing Eric Clapton's late night revelation to him, turned to Ringo and said, "You know, Ringo, I'm in love with your wife."

A long, stunned silence followed. No one had the nerve to speak, everyone waiting to hear how Ringo would respond. Visibly upset, but keeping his head, he flicked the ashes off his cigarette into an ashtray. At last he turned to George. "Better you than someone we don't know."

Pattie fled to another room, accompanied by Chris. Maureen showed up after a few minutes and asked if they wanted another drink. For the rest of the evening, everyone pretended that the event had never happened.[15]

On July 4, 1974, Pattie decided that her marriage with George had become a sham. She left him and went to California to stay with her sister Jenny and Jenny's husband, Mick Fleetwood. Eric Clapton learned the news several days later. He phoned and asked Pattie to come and join him while he toured, which she quickly did.

Harrison accepted the transition with stoic detachment, preferring that Pattie go off to live with his friend rather than with someone he might consider unworthy. The next time the three of them met, Clapton felt awkward and anxious and tried to apologize. George shrugged it off. He said with a laugh, "Well, I suppose I'd better divorce her." Clapton was relieved and grateful to have the tense situation resolved by Harrison's gracious acceptance.

George and Pattie would reach an amicable divorce in 1977. Two years later, when George attended a wedding reception for Pattie and Eric, he introduced himself to the other guests as the "husband-in-law."[16]

9

Bangladesh

avi Shankar had started work on an autobiographical film, *Raga*, in the late sixties. George offered to take part, and in June 1971, after completing the major task of writing, recording, and promoting his first solo album, he traveled to California to make good on his promise. He found his friend disturbed by news from Asia.

Some of Ravi's kinsmen lived in East Pakistan, just across the border from the Indian state of Bengal. Three months earlier, East Pakistan had declared its independence. The region was part of India until 1947, when the British gave up trying to hold on to their colony and granted it freedom. Being heavily Muslim, East Pakistan joined West Pakistan in splitting off from mainly Hindu India—even though the two halves of the nation were separated geographically by a thousand miles. As decades passed, the Bengali-speaking residents of the east grew estranged from their Urdu-speaking countrymen to the west. A 1962 constitution, created under martial law, declared that the nation's capital, the army, and the executive branch of government all would be located in West Pakistan—this in spite of the fact that East Pakistan was more populous. In the years that followed, residents of the east began to feel like second-class citizens in their own country. When elections were held in 1970 and 1971, they voted in massive numbers for the party of a reformist Bengali, Mujibur Rahman. He won handily and should have assumed office as prime minister of the entire nation, but the leader of the party he was replacing and the Pakistani army refused to accept his win. Public resistance began. When the army tried to break the East

Pakistanis' spirit by taking Rahman into custody, his party declared independence and renamed East Pakistan as Bangladesh. Fighting broke out, and the army responded savagely. Hundreds of thousands of people were slaughtered or died of disease. Ten million refugees poured across the border into India, where they were isolated in camps with insufficient food and unsanitary conditions.[1]

Despite the magnitude of the catastrophe, most people in the West remained ignorant of it. Some, given time, could possibly locate India on a world map—but where, they wondered, was *East* Pakistan? Much more pressing at the time was the question, What did Richard Nixon know about the Watergate break-in and when did he know it? Who *cared* what was happening on the far side of the planet?

Ravi cared. When his kinsmen wrote to him of their ordeal, he felt moved to help. He came up with the idea of a benefit concert and appealed to George to take part, hoping to raise ten to twenty thousand dollars. Stirred by his friend's pain and the plight of millions of anonymous people on the other side of the world, George agreed—but thought bigger. With the memory of Woodstock still fresh in mind, Harrison envisioned a world-class concert with noble intentions—the brightest lights in the world of rock music all subduing their egos, and forgoing their paychecks, to help fellow human beings they didn't even know. Every penny of income—from the gate receipts to the profits from an album and a film—would go toward alleviating suffering.[2]

To start the ball rolling Harrison set about writing a song to call attention to the calamity. But that was simply what came naturally. In this case he knew he would have to do more. In spite of his distaste for the limelight, he felt a need to overcome his natural reserve, his preference for being one member of a group. The rolling wheel of fate had placed *George Harrison* at the center of a web connecting hordes of suffering people with musicians whose talents could persuade more fortunate people to save them. *His* turn had come. Just as John Lennon—who was in many ways George's role model—had gotten personally involved and made use of his fame to advance the cause of peace, George decided that he would have to put himself on the line to help the people of Bangladesh.

He reserved Madison Square Garden for August 1, 1971, and committed himself to producing a show unlike any that had ever taken place. He began calling everyone he knew in the business. First, of course, he turned to his three oldest friends, thinking that in spite of the strained relations the other ex-Beatles might set aside their squabbles to help. Only Ringo would not disappoint him. Paul, bitter over a countersuit the three had filed against him, replied that he would perform only if they agreed to drop it. John, who had blazed the trail, found the idea appealing; however, he now considered Yoko Ono as much a part of him as his right arm. When George made clear that the invitation was for him alone, Lennon found himself in an untenable situation and impetuously hopped a jet for Europe to remove himself from the crossfire. Ringo, ever the dependable mate, answered the summons—even though it meant interrupting the filming of a movie.

George's close friend Eric Clapton felt a strong desire to accept George's invitation but was so addicted to heroin that he knew he would be unable to perform without it. To bring the drug into the United States with him was too risky, which meant trying to find a source when he arrived. Even so, he agreed to come.

Harrison had been about to produce an album in England for the group Badfinger. He apologized for having to postpone but asked if they would like to take part in the concert. They accepted. He also confirmed such other old friends as Klaus Voormann and Billy Preston.

Of all the stars Harrison hoped to include in the concert, none—with the possible exception of John Lennon—would bring greater cachet than Bob Dylan. Always a withdrawn and enigmatic figure, he had become even more so in the years following his motorcycle accident in the summer of 1966. He had emerged from his self-imposed exile only for a Carnegie Hall tribute to Woody Guthrie in January 1968 and for the Isle of Wight Festival in August 1969. George appealed to Dylan as a personal friend and stressed the noble purpose of the concert. Even so, Dylan was evasive. He said he would consider the invitation seriously but would not make a commitment.

As the event neared, Harrison needed to get to New York to organize rehearsals. The flight he took from Los Angeles was without doubt the most terrifying of his life. Not only did his aircraft nearly collide with a Boeing 707, it blundered into an electrical storm. The plane bounced around frantically, dropped hundreds of feet in seconds, and was struck by lightning *three* times. At one point George believed the rear of the plane had been blown off. He coped by cinching his seatbelt as tight as he could, pressing his feet against the seat in front of him, and yelling out the Hare Krishna mantra for the better part of two hours. When the aircraft landed safely in New York, he gave the mantra full credit for bringing him through the ordeal.

The musicians started to gather. They had just five days to map out and fine-tune a show that would be the focus of the eyes of the world. George was pleased to see that Dylan showed up for rehearsals, but he was still too skittish about performing to commit to appearing at the actual event. Clapton arrived from England but remained in his hotel room. He had arranged for a supply of heroin to be waiting for him but learned that the deal had fallen through. While his girlfriend dashed around the city in a dangerous search to locate some, Eric began to suffer through the agony of withdrawal. Just as it seemed that he would have to let Harrison down, one of the concert cameramen gave him some methadone he was taking for an ulcer. Meanwhile, excitement was building. The historic performance sold out so quickly that a second show was added for the same date.

On August 1, prepared or not, the ensemble took the stage at noon. Harrison opened the program with an introduction of Ravi Shankar, bowing respectfully to the maestro. As Ravi and his group took their places and tuned their instruments, the proceedings got off to an awkward start. Being unfamiliar with Indian music, the audience misunderstood when, after a minute or two, the musicians all paused in their tuning to prepare to begin the piece. The silence was broken by a round of polite applause. Ravi thanked the crowd and acknowledged the mistake with a smile: "If you appreciate our tuning so much, I hope you will enjoy the playing more."

After half an hour of Indian music, George came on and performed "Wah Wah," "Something," and "Awaiting on You All." He served as emcee and participant for several following acts, then had the stage cleared and played an evocative and warmly received rendition of "Here Comes the Sun."

Due up next was Bob Dylan. Harrison glanced offstage, uncertain to the last whether the skittish superstar would appear. Relieved, he saw Dylan standing in the wings, fidgeting and wielding his guitar, with a harmonica holder fixed around his neck. "I'd like to bring on a friend of us all," Harrison said. "Mr. Bob Dylan." Like a sphinx emerging from a cavern, the reclusive genius came out into the light and launched into "A Hard Rain's Gonna Fall," followed by several other signature songs.

Harrison ended the show with a rousing version of the song he had written especially for the occasion, "Bangla Desh."[3]

By any measure, the concert was a triumph. Financially, the effort caused funds and assistance to flow to the hapless victims—even if much of the aid became mired in tax problems and the miserliness of corporations that profited from the artists' work. But as Harrison would point out later, the money raised was important but secondary. What mattered was that, in just one afternoon and evening, the word "Bangladesh" was implanted in the consciousness of the world. As Harrison foresaw, the media reveled in the gathering of rock royalty and characterized the spectacle as history making. Because of its positioning as a humanitarian effort, all descriptions of the show included a summary of the catastrophe in South Asia. Overnight, because of their fascination with rock stars, masses of people became educated about geopolitical events they had not even been aware of the week before. The tragedy in Bangladesh moved to the fore as an international issue.

When the concert album was released, Harrison had a second, successive triple album under his belt—a mammoth hit that would win the Grammy for Album of the Year.

The Concert for Bangladesh sealed Harrison's stature as something more than just a major celebrity. Just as John Lennon had set the precedent for political and social engagement by rock stars, blazing the trail for such figures as Bono, George had shown that music had more to offer than just entertainment, paving the way for Live Aid, Farm Aid, and other such all-star humanitarian events. He changed the perception of recording artists, making it clear they could be good world citizens too—willing to set aside their egos and paychecks in order to help people who were suffering.

As George himself had pointed out, all things must pass. After the elation of the moment died down, the somewhat-less-than-ideal world intruded again. In his haste to put together an event that had never been done before, Harrison had neglected to register as a tax-exempt organization. The Internal Revenue Service expected its portion of the profits. And while the artists had all generously agreed to waive their royalties, Capitol EMI Music Worldwide wanted reimbursement of its costs to distribute the album—to the tune of $400,000. Irate, George appealed to the US government to make an exception and threatened to release the album through Capitol EMI's chief competitor. In November he went on Dick Cavett's television program to make public his headaches and issued an open challenge to the head of Capitol EMI, Bhaskar Menon: "Sue me, Bhaskar!" When the album was issued in the United Kingdom he faced further problems with Inland Revenue. In July 1973, exasperated, he wrote the ministry his personal check for one million pounds.[4]

The Concert for Bangladesh served as a vindication of the spiritual path Harrison was following. For some reason he could not fathom, karmic law had bestowed on him wealth, fame, and great influence.

Employing that gift for noble purposes, he was helping to reduce suffering and to create goodwill among people who did not even know each other. The favorable response to the concert, coming on the heels of his success with *All Things Must Pass*—which had made public his reverence for Krishna—made him feel rewarded and energized.

10

Closet Yogi

Despite his stature as an A-list celebrity, someone who could summon the world's media with a simple phone call, someone who could impact the lives of people on the other side of the planet, George Harrison retained a working-class view of life. Joey Molland, a member of Badfinger, commented: "One thing you'd learn about George very early was that if you talked to him like he was a Beatle, he would close up and walk away. If you talked to him like he was a regular bloke, . . . then he'd be all ears and get right into it with you."[1]

Harrison had an effective way to remain "grounded"—he was a gardener. His brother Peter, who helped maintain the grounds at Friar Park, called George "a fanatic" about gardening, and George would dedicate his autobiography, *I Me Mine*, "to gardeners everywhere." His passion for cultivating plants and vegetation began in childhood, when he worked alongside his father. The back garden at his first home on Arnold Grove consisted of a one-foot strip of hard ground surrounded by concrete, but when the family moved to a more spacious residence in the suburb of Speke, his father started two gardens—one in front of the house and one in back. There he planted beans, cabbages, and potatoes as well as such flowers as goldenrod and lupines. George's childhood was filled with memories of toiling under the summer sun, coming inside with soiled knees and a sweaty collar, cleaning dirt from beneath his fingernails. That was one reason he found Friar Park so fulfilling. Compared with the tiny gardens in Speke, it was like Disney World—a seemingly endless fantasyland where he could satisfy his urge to interact with nature. Although he employed a full-time crew to keep up the grounds, he loved to don overalls and boots and join them—digging, planting, and pruning for his own enjoyment.

Konrad Engbers, the owner of a nursery in the vicinity of Friar Park, recalled the first time George came to his stall in the market. "How are things going?" George asked. "A little slow," Engbers replied. "I'll give it a little push for you," George said, and purchased almost every tree he had on hand. Even so, George never expected preferential treatment whenever he returned to Engbers's stall. He would stand in line and wait his turn. Engbers marveled: "Such a kind man, with no airs and graces—a man with a truly big heart."[2]

Still, this "regular bloke" had some eccentricities. Like many practitioners of japa yoga, he carried his wooden prayer beads with him everywhere. He kept them in a purple satin bag dangling from a strap around his neck. That enabled him to meditate surreptitiously, fingering them while silently reciting mantras. Those unfamiliar with the bag misunderstood. Some assumed he had hurt his hand and was keeping it protected or hidden in the bag. So many asked him that eventually he grew tired of explaining and simply agreed—saying that, yes, he had had an accident. Those who encountered him around Henley might also notice that he wore beads around his neck. Krishna disciples wore them out of custom—beads made from the wood of the tulsi bush, sacred in India. Beginners traditionally wore a single strand. Initiated disciples wore three strands to signify their level of commitment. George wore two strands.

A "closet yogi" was how he referred to himself, at least among those who shared his religious views. He was an ardent believer, yet he lived a conventional life. He fretted over whether his secular lifestyle might appear to be a lack of commitment to his faith, so he asked Swami Prabhupada whether he thought he should shave his head and move in with the community. The Swami reassured him, saying that being a celebrity and songwriter greatly benefited the advancement of Krishna consciousness.[3]

As a closet yogi, Harrison went through the motions of living in the material world in the same way an individual today might take part in a virtual-reality game.

Sophisticated virtual-reality games did not exist during Harrison's lifetime. However, they provide a useful analogy now. We take for granted that our everyday world and the people with whom we interact are what they appear to be—but what if they are not? Entertain, for a moment, the idea that each of us is a participant in some vast virtual-reality game. Imagine that our souls chose, at the time of our birth, the avatars we now think of as ourselves. Harrison alludes to the concept in the introductory note he wrote for Prabhupada's book *KRSNA*: "With many lives our association with the TEMPORARY has grown. This impermanent body, a bag of bones and flesh, is mistaken for our true self, and we have accepted this temporary condition to be final."[4]

In our ignorance, we believe that we are the bodies we see when we look in a mirror and that we are interacting with other people like us. But what if, in reality, we are interacting with other souls also inhabiting avatars? According to mainstream Hindu belief, we go through our lives believing we are experiencing everything for the first and only time, but actually we are in the process of working out our karmic imbalances from previous incarnations. Since we fail to understand why we are here, we often make more poor choices and have to deal with the consequences of our newest actions. (*Karma* is Sanskrit for "action.") So we keep coming back again and again. On the other hand, we *can* balance out the negative impact of past actions by positive actions in this life, and the correction does not need to be quid pro quo. We can choose to do something, or choose not to do something, simply out of altruism—heedless of our own self-interest. This action redresses some of the imbalance we have brought with us into this life. The goal of the "game" is to reach a state in which our actions are no longer motivated by self-interest and desire. The aim is to overcome our ego and become a serene, wise, neutral observer.

Pursuing further the analogy of the virtual-reality game, what we see and experience during the game appears to be real. But if we lift ourselves out of the avatar's point of view, we realize we are *not* the avatar, but the entity that chose to enter *that* specific body at *that* specific point in time. So what we see and experience during the game is actually an illusion. The Sanskrit word for this beguiling illusion is *maya*.

From this enlightened perspective, we can choose to look at our experiences in the world in a very objective way. Our ups and downs, our joys and tribulations, are not happening to us at all but to our avatar this time around. We can still appreciate our life experiences, only not let them affect us too deeply. "The danger is when you become attached too possessively to each other," Harrison declared, "even to your own body, or to your wealth, your motorcars, your fame, your fortune. The idea is to become unattached to it but still experience it."[5]

The tense relations with the other Beatles, the lawsuits flying back and forth, the vicious barbs of music critics, the complaints of disappointed fans—all lose their sharp edge. They become less upsetting, more a nuisance.

However, dislocating the ego this way can also have awkward ramifications. Consider George's relationship with Pattie. According to Eric Clapton's version of events, when he finally summoned the nerve to confront George with the fact that he loved Pattie, he asked with trepidation, "What are you going to do about it?" George's response shocked him: "Whatever you like, man. It doesn't worry me. You can have her and I'll have your girlfriend." For Harrison, who was firmly convinced we are all temporary visitors to this material world, it mattered little in the great scheme of things if his wife moved on to be with his friend during one particular incarnation. Later in the same year, when asked by an interviewer about the breakup, he replied, "In this life, there is no time to lose in an uncomfortable situation."[6]

What *does* matter in the great scheme of things is to wake up from the dreamlike state we mistake for reality. According to Hindu belief, realizing the truth about ourselves is essential. God permeates every atom of the universe—*all* is divine. Therefore, the truth we are too distracted to recognize is that each of us has the spark of divinity within.

Swami Vivekananda, one of the Indian sages whose writings most influenced Harrison, made the point in his *Raja Yoga*: "Each soul is potentially divine. The goal is to manifest this divinity within by controlling nature, external and internal." George accepted Vivekananda's words about universal divinity the moment he read them. He had never been satisfied with the doctrine he had been handed as a child. Jesus had stated in John 10:30, "I and the Father are one," and the Roman Catholic Church accordingly insisted that Jesus alone was the Son of God and so entitled to the worship of countless generations of later mortals. "I was raised Catholic," Harrison later said, "but even as a kid I couldn't understand the claim that Jesus was the only Son of God when, in fact, we all are."[7]

To Harrison, Jesus was a fully realized incarnation of God—but so were Rama, Buddha, Babaji, and other spiritual masters of India. The miracles Jesus performed were like the miracles *they* performed. Jesus was a poor Galilean who had awakened to his divinity and awed the masses with his powers. He was worthy of veneration, but there was nothing unique about him. He was the Son of God to the same degree that we are *all* children of God. Any enlightened person could do what he had done, and in fact the point of being in this world was to reach that goal.

As great souls such as Vivekananda and Yogananda made clear, the reward at the end of the road was there for everyone. The key was to awaken and get started on the path.

Some might find enlightenment through the guiding hand of a guru. To others it might come through the discipline of yoga. Some might employ meditation, some chanting. Harrison explored them all. However, he found chanting particularly satisfying and efficacious—both in the form of japa yoga (or individual) devotion and *kirtana* (or congregational) singing. He had been impressed initially by the public chanting he heard when accompanying Ravi Shankar around India in late 1966. Upon his return to England, he happened upon the album Swami Prabhupada had recorded in New York to introduce Krishna Consciousness to the West. Fascinated by the album, George played it for John Lennon, and they started to chant regularly—most notably the Hare Krishna mantra (or maha-mantra). When Krishna Consciousness members came to England to start a branch, Harrison visited them to chant with them. And when he moved into Friar Park he invited some to come and live with him so they could chant together.

Regular meditation through chanting and the use of japa beads brought him a sense of "buoyancy" and "energy" and helped him to cope with the vexations of daily life. In the words of the Bhagavad Gita, he strove to become "situated in transcendence." The Gita explains (5:20–21): "Such a liberated person is not attracted to material sense pleasure but is always in trance, enjoying the pleasure within. In this way the self-realized person enjoys unlimited happiness, for he concentrates on the Supreme."[8]

People who knew George uniformly spoke of him as compassionate, genuine, and content in his beliefs. Joel Dorn, an executive for Atlantic and A&M Records who produced five Grammy-winning records, was typical, saying that he saw true humility in Harrison and that he was not so much interested in preaching his faith as in finding comfort in its essence.

When George did try to communicate to others his good feelings, especially in the decade of the seventies, his efforts were often misinterpreted. "You can go through life, go through millions of lives, and not even catch on to what the purpose is. . . . That is, I suppose, why I wrote some songs that were trying to say: 'Hey, you can all experience this, it's available for everyone.' But then you realise you can take the horse to the water, but you can't make him drink. . . . And people only get it when they're ready to get it. Sometimes people took the songs the wrong way, as if I was trying to preach, but I wasn't."[9]

Harrison attributed much of his good feeling to the practice of chanting the maha-mantra. When the Beatles traveled to Greece in July 1967,

George and John stood on the deck of their ship for hours with ukulele banjos, chanting the maha-mantra to the sky and wind and sea. "Like six hours we sang, because we couldn't stop once we got going. As soon as we stopped, it was like the lights went out. It went on to the point where our jaws were aching, singing the mantra over and over and over and over and over. We felt exalted; it was a very happy time for us." He later explained in an interview with his Krishna Consciousness friend Mukunda Goswami: "The word *Hare* is the word that calls upon the energy that's around the Lord. If you say the *mantra* enough, you build up an identification with God. God's all happiness, all bliss, and by chanting His names we connect with Him."[10]

No one knows how long ago Sanskrit chants were created, but their origins likely go back over four thousand years. It seems reasonable that resonating sounds have an effect on cerebrospinal fluid and on our brains as they float in it. The rishis of ancient India may well have realized this and composed phrases emphasizing certain sequences of vowel sounds and consonants to take advantage of the fact. When a person chants properly, vibrations radiate from his or her vocal chords and nasal chamber—especially to the adjacent spinal column.

According to Indian tradition, chanting is more than just a means of relieving stress and achieving calm. It is a way to redirect the brain's attention away from its material surroundings. It is a well-traveled shortcut to the mystical world. Traditional Indian medicine maintains that an ethereal body coexists in the same space as our physical body. Rising along the spine of this ethereal form, from the tailbone to the crown of the head, is a series of power centers known as chakras. Properly stimulated and attuned, these centers channel the energy of the universe into the enlightened individual. With proper control of this energy, the individual can perform seemingly supernatural feats. Harrison was well aware of this, writing in his autobiography: "A mantra is mystical energy encased in a sound structure, and each mantra contains within its vibrations a certain power. . . . [Mantras] turn the mind toward concentration on the supreme, releasing spiritual energy in the Chakras of the

Body." Therefore, he believed that directed meditation through regular chanting enabled him to achieve a higher level of awareness.[11]

But it was more than just a matter of *belief*. He wrote in his introductory note to Swami Prabhupada's book on Krishna: "If there's a God, I want to see Him. It's pointless to believe in something without proof, and Krishna Consciousness and meditation are methods where you can actually obtain GOD perception. You can actually see God, and hear Him, play with Him. It might sound crazy, but He is actually there, actually with you."[12]

Throughout his life as a closet yogi, chanting served as Harrison's conduit to the mystical world, his favored method of remaining God-conscious and accruing good karma. In a conversation with Mukunda Goswami, he likened life to a piece of string with knots tied in it. The knots represent a person's karma from previous lives, and the object of a person's life is to untie the knots already there in order to be free. However, not being aware of that fact, people tend to create more knots while failing to untie the previous ones. Chanting and God-consciousness, Harrison believed, have the power to untie the knots. The key is accepting the truth of the old axiom "As you sow, so shall you reap." We have no one to blame but ourselves for the situation in which we now find ourselves, but on the other hand we can earn our way back to daylight in the future through positive actions now. And positive action can be as simple as chanting. As Harrison says in "Awaiting on You All," "But here's a way for you to get free / By chanting the names of the Lord and you'll be free."[13]

11

A Long Way from OM

n February 1973 Harrison deepened his commitment to his Hare Krishna friends. He purchased a seventeen-acre estate in Hertfordshire and donated it to the International Society of Krishna Consciousness. The society renamed the mock-Tudor mansion Bhaktivedanta Manor and made it the United Kingdom headquarters of ISKCON.[1]

George also continued his effort to spread awareness of Krishna with his third album as an ex-Beatle, titled *Living in the Material World*, released in May 1973. The album expresses his impressions of the mundane and the spiritual worlds and the importance of ignoring the lures of the everyday world and remaining focused on the eternal verities. Not that he would ever have viewed himself in their company, but he had just turned thirty, the age when Buddha left his palace to seek the truth and Jesus confronted the authorities at Jerusalem.

The first track of his new album was "Give Me Love (Give Me Peace on Earth)," a bouncy yet soothing tune that would have slipped nicely into *All Things Must Pass*. Just as he had deftly incorporated the Hare Krishna mantra into "My Sweet Lord," he worked the sacred word *OM* into "Give Me Love," stretching out the syllable for several bars on the way to delivering the phrase "My Lord."

In the title track, he compares "sweet memories" of the "Spiritual Sky" with the frustrations and never-quite-gratified senses of the material world. He refers metaphorically to his incarnation in the world: "Use my body like a car, / Taking me both near and far." And he speaks of final escape from it: "I hope to get out of this place / by the Lord Sri

Krishna's Grace." As he would later summarize his view of life in the material world, "The whole point to being here, really, is to figure a way to get out."[2]

"The Lord Loves the One (That Loves the Lord)" was written following a conversation with his spiritual mentor of the time, A. C. Bhaktivedanta Swami Prabhupada. In it he lays out his belief that "the Lord helps those that help themselves." That is, the surest way to merit Krishna's grace is to earn it through devotion to him. "The law says if you don't give, / then you don't get loving."

While *Living in the Material World* did have secular moments ("Sue Me, Sue You Blues"), for the most part it revolved around Harrison's spirituality and made a fine companion piece to *All Things Must Pass*. The cover art featured a Kirlian photograph (taken by a UCLA parapsychologist) of George's hand, with a Hindu medallion in his palm. The album raced to the top of the US charts and reached number three in the United Kingdom, selling three million copies worldwide.[3]

In early 1974, uncomfortable at home with Pattie and feeling the need for solitude, George traveled alone to the south coast of France. There he rented a car and began to drive. He drove straight across northern Spain and into Portugal, chanting the maha-mantra the entire time—twenty-three hours without a break.[4]

In February he returned to India with Ravi Shankar. Once more they visited Vrindavan, where tradition had it that Krishna had lived thousands of years ago. Ravi told George he had arranged for them to meet a famous holy man there, Sripad Maharaj. On arriving in town, they stopped first to share tea with a barefoot man with long matted hair, who was dressed in beggar's clothing. Ravi chatted with him briefly in some native tongue. When the man invited them out to walk, they followed, George assuming he was escorting them to the holy man. The truth dawned on him as everyone they encountered prostrated themselves to touch the simple man's feet. Everywhere, that evening and all through the night, the residents of Vrindavan chanted and sang praise to Krishna. The following morning Maharaj showed Harrison the ancient park where Krishna had danced and played his flute. Afterward, the ragged holy man led devotees in a call-and-response song. George chanted along with the others for hours, his eyes closed in utter bliss, not wanting the experience to end.[5]

Upon his return to England, he contemplated what to do next. He was riding a wave of success since leaving the Beatles, and his visit to Krishna's holy city had invigorated him, much as a visit to Jerusalem might invigorate a devout Christian or Jew. (In his autobiography he referred to it as "my most fantastic experience.") When he began to think of his next album, he toyed with the idea of a US tour to support it—an idea sure to spark excitement since no ex-Beatle had toured America. He thought back to the Bangladesh concert. In it he had integrated a segment of classical Indian music into the performance, and the crowd had accepted the novelty. What if he could move past that beach-head? What if he devoted a portion of each concert to Ravi and his musicians and instilled in the minds of those who came to hear Beatle George an appreciation for the music he loved? In the Bangladesh benefit, he had also performed songs with spiritual content—"Awaiting on You All," urging the listener to chant the names of the Lord to become free; "Beware of Darkness," warning of the seductive power of maya; and his megahit "My Sweet Lord," featuring the Hare Krishna mantra. Why not carry the idea further and proselytize? How many hearts and minds attracted by the aura of the Beatles could be turned toward what really mattered—Krishna?

Why settle for being a performing flea when he could be a force for good? If he could bring the millennia-old wisdom to the attention of the crowds who came to hear him, the curiosity of some listeners might be sparked. Perhaps many of them would go on to learn more about meditation or yoga or Yogananda or the Gita. One tour might open tens of thousands of minds to the wisdom found in Eastern mysticism. He had visions of masses of young people awakening from their love affair with maya and beginning to transform themselves. He once told his friend Mukunda: "The truth is there. It's right within us all. Understand what you are. If people would just wake up to what's real, there would be no misery in the world."[6]

He issued an announcement in March that he planned to tour America that fall. As he anticipated, the announcement met with a groundswell of interest. Unfortunately, the shimmering vision in his mind did not translate into the real world. His first misstep was in waiting too long to begin writing and recording material. He came up with a title for the album, *Dark Horse*, but developed laryngitis when it came time to record the songs for it and could not take a break to rest his voice. Committed to a seven-week schedule of concerts for which he was not fully prepared, he left for the United States with the album unfinished. He further aggravated his condition during rehearsals, and when the tour began, the quality of his voice declined with each performance. Worse, the reaction to the juxtaposition of Indian and Western sets was not as warm as he hoped. His appeals regarding Krishna left many in the audience feeling harangued when they had come to be entertained.

Critics began to refer to the George Harrison & Friends tour as his "Dark Hoarse" tour and compared his voice to Bob Dylan's "on an off night." George had been present at some of Dylan's tumultuous United Kingdom concerts in 1966, when the crowd booed and yelled "Judas!" as they saw him take the stage with an electric guitar and a backup band instead of his acoustic guitar. Dylan, determined to go his own way and let the chips fall where they might, had simply turned to his rock band and directed, "Play louder!" Harrison was no less determined to remain true to himself. If he recoiled from criticism, what would it say about his commitment to his beliefs? So he called out to the crowd appealing to them to chant "Hare Hare" and "Krishna! Christ! Krishna! Christ!" then chastised them when they didn't respond with enough enthusiasm. "I don't know what you think, but from up here you sound pretty dead." To another listless audience he remarked, "I'm not up here jumping like a loony for my own sake but to tell you that the Lord is in your hearts. Somebody's got to tell you." Determined to distance himself from the Beatles legend, he resisted including Beatles songs in his playlist, and when at last he relented in order to please the audience, he changed the lyrics. Covering John Lennon's "In My Life," he sang that he "loved *God* more"; and his guitar didn't gently weep, it "smiled." Even when large parts of the audience began to stream out, he kept on employing the stage as a pulpit. He ended every show with the same benediction: "All glories to Sri Krishna!"[7]

Not in good health when he began the tour, Harrison further depleted his physical and mental strength with every passing week. Upon his return to Friar Park at the end of the tour, he walked, zombie-like, around the gardens. "That was the nearest I got to a nervous breakdown. I couldn't even go into the house." Still, he was satisfied that the tour represented some kind of victory. Despite negative reviews and his substandard vocals, despite his driving himself to the edge of a breakdown, hundreds of thousands of people had been exposed to Indian music and Krishna consciousness. What disappointed him were the kinds of people who had come out for his shows. Every day was a spiritual quest for him; he might fall short, but he made a conscious effort to love God and his people and his world. The "fans" who had come to see Harrison did not exhibit such lofty aims. "I'd go out there onstage and you'd just get stoned because there was so much reefer going about. I just thought, 'Do I actually have anything in common with these people?'"[8]

At the beginning of the tour, while addressing the media in Los Angeles, he had described the undertaking as a test case. He said either he would be "ecstatically happy" when it finished and want to tour everywhere, or he would go back to his "cave" again for five years. As it turned out, the return to his cave would extend to seventeen years.[9]

One bright spot in the problematic year was Olivia Trinidad Arias. Born in Mexico City in 1948, she had moved to California in her youth along with her family. Working as a secretary at A&M Records in 1974, she was hired for the Los Angeles office of George's new label, Dark Horse Records. First on the telephone, and later in person, George came to find her charming and uplifting. He enjoyed her company so much that he made sure she accompanied him on his tour, and their relationship blossomed. After the tour she traveled with him on vacation to Hawaii, and from there she moved in with him at Friar Park.

Nineteen seventy-five started off with new legal problems. Bright Tunes Music Corporation, which held the copyright to "He's So Fine" and had alleged as early as March 1971 that the melodies from "My Sweet Lord" were lifted from the 1960s hit, finally took the issue to court. Bright Tunes claimed copyright infringement and said it was entitled to the enormous royalties generated. Harrison countered that his inspiration had been "Oh Happy Day" by the Edwin Hawkins Singers. The case would drag on for well over a year, with George required to give testimony in court, and ultimately he would lose the battle. In September 1976 the judge declared that the two songs were substantially the same, and that Harrison had subconsciously plagiarized the sixties hit. Ultimately, George would resolve the affair by purchasing Bright Tunes and thus owning the rights to both songs.

From late 1973, when news reports of the Harrisons' marital troubles began to circulate, through 1974 and into 1975, George suffered through what he termed in his autobiography "the naughty period." Battered by the world, with Pattie having her own affairs and then moving out, with his glittering vision for a great tour being dashed and his *Dark Horse* album being savaged by critics and floundering in the charts, Harrison swirled down into a spiritual funk. He slipped back into his worldly ways, admitting in an interview in September 1975, "Compared to what I should be, I'm a heathen."[10]

For what would be his final album under the old contract with EMI, he delivered *Extra Texture: Read All About It*. The apparently whimsical title turned out to be darkly sarcastic, as the album was filled with downbeat tracks. The darkest was "Grey Cloudy Lies" with its reference to a "pistol at my brain." He sings of only wanting to live "with no teardrops in my eyes," but there seems to be "no chance." In "World of Stone" he advises those who are wise not "to follow the like of me." Where does he find himself? "Such a long way from home," he says, but in his autobiography he renders it, "Such a long way from OM"—confessing his inner turmoil at having strayed from his faith. "Tired of Midnight Blue" is a long allusion to his visit to a club in Los Angeles and his revulsion to the decadence he had witnessed there—"Made me chill right to the bone." He had reached rock bottom.

In contrast, the songs on his next album, *Thirty-Three & 1/3*, suggest a recommitment to his spiritual life. The title is a pun—he was that age at the time of recording, and vinyl LPs of the time played at 33 1/3 revolutions per minute.

Much had happened in the year since *Extra Texture*. Harrison's health had continued to deteriorate. He tried chanting his way to vitality using techniques specified in *Scientific Healing Affirmations*, a book by one of his icons, Paramahansa Yogananda. When that failed to benefit him, he gave in to Olivia's appeals and went to a doctor. The diagnosis came back: serious liver damage and hepatitis, obviously due to his years of abusing alcohol and drugs. George gave up both and was put on a vitamin regimen. When he still failed to improve, Olivia searched for other solutions. She finally contacted Dr. Zion Yu, an acupuncture wizard who had treated her brother Peter following a motorcycle accident. Skeptical at first, George finally relented and they traveled to California for a series of treatments. He improved almost immediately and recovered fully in a few months.[11]

Meanwhile, the bout with illness took a toll on his business relationships. When his recording contract with EMI ended in January 1976, Harrison signed with his own label, Dark Horse Records. Contractually, his first post-EMI record was to be distributed by A&M Records, and he committed to deliver the album to them by July 26. When he overshot that deadline by two months, A&M sued him for $10 million.

Thirty-Three & 1/3 came out in November, distributed instead by Warner Bros. The first single from the album was "This Song," a musical jibe at the judicial circus he had endured over the suit filed by Bright Tunes Music. "This tune has nothing 'Bright' about it," he sings. "My expert tells me it's okay." Closer to his heart, however, was "Dear One," a song of love and homage to Paramahansa Yogananda, the Indian mystic whom he acknowledges in his autobiography as "a great influence on my life." Whenever he traveled to the Los Angeles area, George liked to visit the Self-Realization Fellowship retreat in Encinitas, strolling through the spectacular but serene gardens overlooking the Pacific Ocean. Ravi Shankar had performed at the retreat as early as 1957 and maintained a home only three miles away.

Another great influence on George, Swami Prabhupada, founder of the International Society of Krishna Consciousness, passed away in mid-November 1977. Harrison had last seen him in July of the previous year during a visit to Bhaktivedanta Manor. The eighty-one-year-old guru had returned home to India at the end, spending his last days in Vrindavan at a temple devoted to Krishna. On his deathbed, he slipped off a ring he always wore and instructed one of his disciples to give it to George.[12]

After *Thirty-Three & 1/3* Harrison did not release another album for three years. Freed from his contract with EMI and the relentless need to produce and promote new work, he took time off to enjoy life with Olivia.

He became an aficionado of Formula One racing, attending the 1977 British Grand Prix at the Silverstone racecourse. He once said, "Most musicians want to be athletic stars of some sort. My fantasy is to be a race-car driver." He had been in love with fast cars even before he became wealthy enough to afford them and had a penchant for tearing up British highways. He joked that he rated himself good behind the wheel but felt that the police might not agree. In 1963 he had been driving the Beatles' van along an icy road in Yorkshire and took a turn too fast. The van slid down an embankment and crashed through a series of concrete poles, and George subsequently lost his license for three months. In early 1971, for "driving without reasonable consideration," he was banned from driving for a year. Days after the ban expired, on February 28, 1972, he slammed into a roadside crash barrier at ninety miles an hour. He suffered a concussion and had a scalp wound that required eight stitches. Pattie, in the car with him at the time, was worse. She too had a concussion, as well as broken ribs, and had to spend several days in the hospital and two weeks convalescing in a nursing home. When Harrison went to court five months later, he was fined twenty pounds and banned once more from driving. His license would be taken away yet again in October 1979.[13]

Willie Weeks, his bass player during the *Dark Horse* sessions, twice rode with Harrison when they took breaks from recording to drive into Henley-on-Thames for fish-and-chips. The first trip was made in a Ferrari, the second in a Porsche. Both times George turned the winding country road that led from town to his estate into a roaring, sliding, micro Grand Prix. The first trip ended without incident, but on the second George was racing too fast to manage a turn and slammed into hedges lining the side of his driveway. After extricating the Porsche, George gave a sheepish laugh and shrugged his shoulders. Weeks decided to come down on the side of discretion. When they walked into the house, neither mentioned to the other musicians what had happened.[14]

In the late seventies Harrison became a regular at Grand Prix races in Monte Carlo, California, and Australia, as well as Britain. He had become a fan of sports-car racing at the age of twelve, when he attended the British Grand Prix in Liverpool. He wrote a song inspired by the sport, "Faster," and befriended the world's most famous drivers—Stirling Moss, Emerson Fittipaldi, Jackie Stewart, and others. A highlight of his life came when Moss allowed him to don a helmet and uniform and take a lap in Moss's Lotus 18, which had won the 1960 Monte Carlo Grand Prix.

Harrison had been watching when the very first *Monty Python's Flying Circus* program aired on BBC2 in October 1969. He found it so hilarious and innovative that he and Apple press agent Derek Taylor sent the troupe a telegram of encouragement. Over time George met the members and became particularly close with Eric Idle. In December 1975 Idle persuaded him to appear as "Pirate Bob" on his follow-up program to Monty Python, *Rutland Weekend Television*. In another recurring sketch for the program, the Beatles were parodied under the guise of the Rutles (the "Prefab Four"). When Idle expanded the sketch ideas into a "mockumentary" for television, *All You Need Is Cash*, Harrison portrayed a television interviewer questioning a Rutles press agent, who was based on Derek Taylor.[15]

As a result of his friendship with Idle and other members of Monty Python, Harrison was drawn into the making of *Monty Python's Life of Brian*, their follow-up film to *Monty Python and the Holy Grail*. Three days before filming was set to begin in Tunisia, the financial backers reneged on funding. They had decided that the subject matter, a parody of the life of Jesus, was simply too controversial. When the Python players approached George, he cheerfully put up the money. He and a business associate formed HandMade Films for that purpose in September 1978, and the profits he made from *Life of Brian* would finance a series of films over the next two decades. He would later comment on the controversy surrounding the film: "It's only the ignorant people—who didn't care to check it out—who thought that it was knocking Christ. Actually, it was upholding Him and knocking all the idiotic stuff that goes on around religion." Grateful for his rescue of the project (and no doubt thinking of publicity value and box-office appeal), Python members offered George the role of Jesus, who appears early in the film delivering his Sermon on the Mount. But George, avoiding the limelight, settled for a fleeting cameo later on as "Mr. Papadopolous."[16]

On August 1, 1978, George welcomed his own son into the material world. He named him Dhani after two sequential notes on the Indian musical scale, syllables that also—in Sanskrit—create the word "wealthy." A month later, George married Olivia in a private ceremony in Henley-on-Thames. They honeymooned in Tunisia.[17]

George finally began work on songs for a new album. Enjoying the contentment of a quiet domestic life, he felt comfortable just being himself, and he accordingly titled his new project *George Harrison*. The album, released in February 1979, was mellow, serene, and in many ways autobiographical. "Here Comes the Moon"—obviously keying off his famous "Here Comes the Sun"—was inspired by a colorful Hawaiian sunset graced by the simultaneous rising, on the opposite horizon, of a lovely moon. "Dark Sweet Lady," a Spanish-sounding tune, was written to express his love and gratitude to Olivia. "Soft-Hearted Hana" recalled the standard "Hard-Hearted Hannah" but was written following the ingestion of some magic mushrooms on Maui. "Faster" was inspired by his passion for Formula One racing, but the final lyrics were broad enough to suggest intensity in any situation.

Derek Taylor persuaded Harrison to publish his autobiography in 1980. Self-conscious about speaking about himself, he thought the title *I Me Mine* offered just the right touch of irony. An unconventional autobiography, the book was episodic, interlaced with comments from Taylor, and incomplete. Instead of the customary string of chronological recollections, George focused on revelations of his feelings and passions. The narrative comprised only 20 percent of the book's length, much of that italicized interpolations by Taylor. George devoted most of the rest of the book to his music—offering comments on every song he had published to that time, and providing complete lyrics and facsimiles of the papers on which he had written them. Despite its oddities, the book was the first (and, to date, *only*) Beatle autobiography, and created a stir.

Genesis Publications first published *I Me Mine* as an expensive, hand-bound, limited-edition book. One of the early readers was John Lennon. With some pique, John discovered that he—the founder and driving force of the Beatles, the person George had idolized in his youth—was mentioned only fleetingly. Harrison never acknowledged him as a mentor or even as an influence. Lennon didn't hesitate to make public his feelings: "He put a book out privately on his life that, by glaring omission, says that my influence on his life is absolutely zilch and nil. . . . I was just hurt. I was just left out as if I didn't exist."[18]

George's negligence was likely due to the fact that their paths had long since diverged. John had been his role model in their youth. Sharing disappointment over the emptiness of worldly success, they had been united by a hunger to find some new foundation for their lives.

The LSD experience had bonded them as spiritual seekers, giving them a common breakthrough and a common starting point. But from it they drew different lessons. Harrison found God and gradually realized that he preferred to worship him in the guise of Krishna. Lennon found something he likened to God but gradually realized that people are the creators of their own lives.

As the eighties began, George had achieved an enviable balance in his life. He had largely put behind him a dark period and the temptations of a rock-star lifestyle. He was leading an affluent but spiritually oriented life surrounded by a loving wife, a healthy son, and many friends. He was the master of his own career and could compose music, or lie fallow, at his leisure. He also had a satisfying new role as film producer. All of this, and he lived on one of the most beautiful estates in Britain. The new decade stretched out before him as a bright path.

Hours before dawn on December 9, 1980, while he was in bed in Friar Park, deeply asleep, his sister, Louise, telephoned from the United States.

She had just heard a news report about John Lennon.

Suggested Listening

"I Me Mine"
"All Things Must Pass"
"My Sweet Lord"
"Awaiting on You All"
"Give Me Love (Give Me Peace on Earth)"

Part Four

THE INNER LIGHT

12

Heading for the Light

George found it difficult to think the unthinkable. Louise provided only the scant details available from the first news bulletins. Surely John was only wounded? George was shocked and saddened, but he knew he would learn the full story in the morning. Since there was nothing he could do from England, he went back to sleep.

When he awoke again, his world had changed. News that John had been shot four times by a deranged fan, and died before reaching the hospital, struck a blow to George's psyche. A jumble of disturbing memories must have rushed back: the volley of bullets once fired at the Beatles' aircraft as they lifted off from Los Angeles, the heart-stopping "gunfire" during one show in Memphis that turned out to be firecrackers, the death threat in Montreal and the bomb scare in Las Vegas, among a hundred other terrifying incidents over the years; and thousands upon thousands upon thousands of people with manic eyes pressing against barriers. Was John's death perhaps only the first step in some larger plot? When people began to gather outside the front gate of Friar Park, the grounds manager took the precaution of chaining the gates together. The Henley police were summoned and began to patrol the grounds.[1]

Harrison's nervousness in public became even more acute. "At times I flash on it," he admitted, "when people call your name from behind. . . . You don't know who's crackers and who isn't." In times past he had visited pubs in Henley to get out of the house and socialize. One evening three years before, he had even taken his guitar to Row Barge pub and treated the regulars to an impromptu performance. Now he would not even consider going there. Michael Palin of Monty Python witnessed the abrupt change: "We used to have a drink in a pub near his house. He didn't mind going there and mixing with people. After John was shot, that's when things changed. George became quite paranoid. He put barbed wire up around his home and retreated."2

George's relationship with John had been the most strained of any between John and the other ex-Beatles. Ringo remained everybody's mate. Paul and John, though no longer close friends, had met, exchanged telephone calls, and even come near to collaborating again in the mid-seventies. But George had driven a massive wedge between himself and Lennon when he invited Lennon—but not Yoko—to perform at the Concert for Bangladesh, and he suffered for it for the rest of the decade. They exchanged pleasantries when they met at events and as colitigants in court, but Lennon was cool to anything more. Then George barely mentioned him in *I Me Mine*. When George tried calling John at his apartment in the Dakota in August 1980 to assuage his anger, John refused to take the call and never bothered to return it. After the initial shock of John's murder and the media frenzy in its aftermath, George was left with an uneasy conscience about their fractured friendship.

He returned to the challenge of completing his next album. He had worked on it sporadically all year and had delivered it in the fall of 1980 for a planned November release. But Warner Bros. executives were not satisfied with it. They rejected four songs as not commercial enough and insisted that George write new ones to replace them. In the month following Lennon's death, George finished the additional work and put the album to rest. He gave it the title—ironic in view of his renewed reclusiveness—*Somewhere in England.*

"All Those Years Ago" was one of the four replacement tracks. Harrison had written it as a song for Ringo, with a different title and different lyrics. They recorded it together in late November as Ringo prepared his own new album for release. But Ringo decided not to include it. He didn't care for some of the lyrics and thought that the key was too high for his voice.

George took back the song and reworked the lyrics. He kept Ringo's drum track and invited Paul to add backing vocals, so the song became a tribute from the remaining Beatles to their fallen comrade. In the song, George expressed the feelings he wished he had voiced while Lennon was still alive. Their relationship had its ups and downs, but Harrison never stopped admiring him: "Living with good and bad / I always looked up to you." He wanted Lennon to know that he lamented the loss of his voice in the world, even if comparatively few understood him: "You said it all / Though not many had ears." The elegy struck a resonant chord with the public. The song reached number two on the US charts, remained there for three weeks, and became George's biggest hit in a decade.[3]

In another of the songs from *Somewhere in England*, "That which I Have Lost," Harrison acknowledged borrowing ideas from Indian scripture. "It's right out of the Bhagavad Gita. In it I talk about fighting the forces of darkness, limitations, falsehood, and mortality." He refers to being rescued by "a light from Heaven" that opened the bolts of his prison and renewed him. He hopes those listening will be rescued from their own darkness, but they all seem preoccupied: "You're too busy fighting revolutions / That keep you back down in the lower world."[4]

John Lennon had spent his last five years as a househusband, shunning the spotlight and savoring the domestic side of life. After his murder, and perhaps as a consequence of it, George Harrison followed his example. He lived a reclusive existence, seldom going out of the house, gardening endlessly, enjoying Dhani's childhood. He purchased a home near Hana on the island of Maui, and when cold weather gripped England he would escape to his tropical hideaway. But even that was not remote enough. Olivia said, "George was always on a quest to get as far away as he could. We found Hawaii and built a house there. But he wanted to keep going. We went to Tasmania, New Zealand, Australia . . . looking for solitude." A friend in Hawaii, British racing driver Jackie Stewart, told him of a paradise as yet undiscovered by the public—Hamilton Island in Australia. When George investigated and found that so far only one bungalow had been built on the lush island, he bought property and built his own sanctuary on a high cliff overlooking the ocean. His life there was as near to Eden as he would ever get. Olivia remarked that it was "at times like being in a zoo, except we were the ones in the cage, because we'd get monitor lizards, kookaburras, wallabies and snakes at the windows looking in at us."[5]

Harrison's experiences Down Under provided him with a title for his next album—*Gone Troppo*. The phrase was Australian slang for going mad from the tropical climate. The songs on the album were workmanlike, but airy, almost frivolous. They were sufficient to fulfill contractual obligations but far from the inspired work he had produced a decade earlier, upon first leaving the Beatles. Released in the United States in October 1982, *Gone Troppo* reached only number 108 in the *Billboard* charts. Harrison was unfazed. Having experienced all that fame and success had to offer, he did not much care anymore. He did not have a competitive nature, and he made no secret that he did not have the desire or energy to undertake the tedious game of promotion that seemed to be required to make an album a hit in the market. What did matter to him was that the album completed his contract with Warner Bros. Completely free now to go his own way, he would take off five years from the music business.[6]

Friends noticed a change in his demeanor. He grew surly and began to use hashish. Rumors circulated that he had begun womanizing again. The disengagement he felt for the world around him extended to his spiritual life. He had reduced his contact with the Hare Krishna movement after the death of Swami Prabhupada at the end of 1977. Now he continued to chant and meditate privately, but he passed through a decade of estrangement from his ISKCON friends.[7]

In the eyes of the world, George was the moody ex-Beatle jaded with success and withdrawing from social life. In his own mystical view, he was a bit of Krishna temporarily inhabiting a body known as George Harrison. To achieve release from the endless round of reincarnation, it is essential not to become too attached. Evidence of his detachment is apparent in many photographs of Harrison. His lips form a smile, but at the same time his eyes betray a touch of melancholy. The wistfulness comes from a profound conviction that the spectacle surrounding him should not be taken too seriously, and that most of the people he encountered were fated to stumble around in darkness for their entire lives.

Imagine one pensive man sitting on a train that is rumbling along in the darkness. He is just a passenger, like all the rest, and when he takes a break from his own thoughts or from gazing out the window, he interacts with them. Some are happy, some are not, but all are preoccupied—making choices, decisions, plans. What this person knows that they don't is that a few miles down the track a bridge has collapsed. The train is going to plunge into a deep gorge. He can warn the others, but they have no reason to believe him. Their focus is on the pressing concerns of the moment—how they look, what meal they should order, how much time remains until they reach their station. With no way to stop the train or get off, the man has no alternative but to try and enjoy the rest of the journey, in spite of his secret knowledge. However, no matter how pleasant he appears, the people around him detect melancholy in his eyes—a sadness with no apparent cause.

Harrison's melancholy comes through in many of his songs. "While My Guitar Gently Weeps," "Isn't it a Pity," "I Me Mine," "Beware of Darkness," and "All Things Must Pass," among others, reflect a world-weariness that seems out of place in one of the Fab Four.

His reticence and anxiety about exposure to the public made George defensive about his sanctuary in Maui. The terms of his purchase of the estate permitted public access to the beach via a path that crossed his grounds. At one point the path approached within some eighty feet of his house. Nettled by the people coming and going—many of whom paused to try and catch a glimpse of their world-famous neighbor—and fearful that some maniac might take advantage of the proximity to invade his house, he went to court to try to end the access. In August 1983 a judge finally ruled that the pathway should be moved—but only to 125 feet from his house, a judgment that left Harrison fuming.

Despite his discomfort in crowds, he did appear occasionally at selected events. His passion for car racing led him to the Long Beach Grand Prix in March 1983. In May 1984 he visited the Chelsea Flower Show in London, and late in that year he accompanied his old friend Derek Taylor to several events in New Zealand and Australia to support the publication of Taylor's autobiography, *Fifty Years Adrift*. George even made a surprise appearance on stage in Sydney on December 14, to the delight of a crowd attending a Deep Purple concert. He asked lead singer Ian Gillan to introduce him as "Arnold Grove from Liverpool."[8]

In October 1985 he found that he could not pass up a televised salute to one of his childhood idols. In *Carl Perkins and Friends: A Rockabilly Session*—created as a special for British television—he joined Ringo Starr, Eric Clapton, Rosanne Cash, and members of the Stray Cats to pay tribute to the King of Rockabilly. George had loved the sound as a teenager, and as a Beatle sang lead vocal on the Perkins tune "Everybody's Trying to Be My Baby." He reprised it for the program, and also performed Perkins's early hit "Glad All Over."

He stayed involved in filmmaking through the eighties. HandMade Films found a niche producing movies that were comparatively low budget and yet found favor with critics and the public. (A 1999 poll of members of the British film industry would rank three—*Life of Brian*, *Withnail and I*, and *Mona Lisa*—among the one hundred best British films of all time.) In 1986, an opportunity came along that promised to be a major success for the company. *Shanghai Surprise* united the controversial Hollywood newlyweds Sean Penn and Madonna as lead actors in a film set in an exotic locale. The media were attracted to the project, and when rumors began to fly that Penn and Madonna were being disruptive and demanding on set, the race was on to get revealing photos and juicy details. Harrison, who had planned only to write some songs for the project and collaborate on the score, was drawn into the media frenzy, which was the worst he had seen since his days as a Beatle. In the end, the film was savaged by the critics and performed poorly at the box office.[9]

George remained wary about committing to work on a new album. Dispirited by his troubles with *Gone Troppo*, he quietly searched for a producer with whom he could work. After long consideration, he finally settled on Jeff Lynne, a former member of Electric Light Orchestra. With over twenty years in the music business, Lynne had proven himself a talented musician, songwriter, singer, and wizard in the studio. Of equal importance, George felt rapport with him personally. He approached Lynne through a mutual friend, Dave Edmunds, and found that Lynne was anxious to work with him. The two began work in George's studio at Friar Park in early 1987, in agreement that the album should be more market oriented than Harrison's recent music.

Cloud Nine had a brighter tone than any of Harrison's other post-Beatles albums. The change was most evident in the three singles released. The first, "Got My Mind Set on You," was a bouncy remake of an obscure 1962 record by James Ray. The song quickly rose to the top of the charts in the United States and became Harrison's first number one since "Give Me Love (Give Me Peace on Earth)." The second and third singles were both cowritten with Lynne. "When We Was Fab" took an affectionate look back at the days of the Fab Four—"when income tax was all we had." "This Is Love" was a sprightly tune that seemed to refer to a romantic relationship, but offered hints that it signified more. We can overcome problems of "our own creation," it says, "when we use the power provided free to everyone."

Nestled among these soft-rock offerings—and straight-ahead rock-and-roll tracks such as "Wreck of the Hesperus" and "Devil's Radio"—was a more profound song that Harrison himself called "straight out of Yogananda." "Fish on the Sand" alluded to George's feelings for Krishna. Born a Pisces—on February 24—he was himself the metaphorical fish on the sand when he felt estranged from Krishna's love. "If I'm not with you / I'm not so much of a man." "I know that you're a part of me / But it's a must to know that you love me too." Even this song, with its more personal and meaningful lyrics, was delivered in an up-tempo, commercial fashion—with the journeyman assistance of Eric Clapton and Elton John.

When *Cloud Nine* was ready to release, Harrison felt so happy with it that he willingly took part in the interviews and promotional efforts he had found so annoying in the past. He knew they would place him in the limelight again, but rationalized that it would be for only a short while. Issued in October 1987, *Cloud Nine* spent thirty-one weeks on the *Billboard* chart and went platinum in sales.[10]

On January 20, 1988, the Beatles were inducted into the Rock 'n' Roll Hall of Fame. Paul McCartney refused to attend, miffed that after almost two decades the others were still wrangling with him about royalties on the music they created together. He announced that he would feel like a "hypocrite" putting on a happy face beside them at a "fake reunion." With Paul a no-show, George stepped up to accept the award on behalf of the group. He kept his remarks brief, beginning with the lighthearted "I don't have much to say because I'm the Quiet Beatle." For the customary jam at the end of the program, Harrison, Starr, Bob Dylan, Bruce Springsteen, Mick Jagger, Little Richard, and Elton John performed a Lennon-McCartney tune that, ironically, was mainly Paul's—"I Saw Her Standing There."[11]

That May, still buoyed by the success of *Cloud Nine*, George was working in Los Angeles, trying to come up with a new song as a bonus track for a twelve-inch single about to be released in Europe. He phoned Jeff Lynne one day to schedule a songwriting session. At the time, Lynne happened to be producing new albums for Roy Orbison and Tom Petty. When George dropped by they all went to dinner together, and when he discussed the project Orbison and Petty offered to help him out. While considering where to go to write and record the song, George suggested they all go to "Bob's house." "Bob" turned out to be Bob Dylan, who maintained a home in Malibu and had installed a studio in his garage. George phoned to arrange the visit, and Dylan answered on the first ring and invited them over.

Thus it was that five of the top recording artists in the world—stars from the fifties, sixties, seventies, and eighties—assembled on one fateful afternoon.

After Dylan welcomed them, he began preparing a barbecue. Harrison and Lynne sat down to start brainstorming. George happened to notice a cardboard box shoved behind a garage door. The words "Handle with Care" caught his attention. With no more inspiration than that, some of the most fertile minds in the music business began to collaborate. Harrison came up with the first line, "Been beat up and battered 'round." The others began to throw in following lines. The song quickly began to take shape. With Roy Orbison on hand, George wanted to write a chorus that would take advantage of his incomparable voice. Soon they were all taking part, and the song went beyond the point where it could be consigned to the B side of a single. The collaboration gave them all such pleasure that they began to think of recording an entire album together.

They faced two complications: Orbison was in the midst of a tour; Dylan was about to begin one. Under pressure, but rich with talent and with decades of experience to draw from, the all-star quintet wrote and recorded ten songs in nine days, and a new supergroup was born.

Naming the group presented another challenge. While working on *Cloud Nine* together, Harrison and Lynne had started to respond to minor mistakes with the comment, "We'll bury it in the mix." As the sessions went on, "We'll bury" transformed into "Wilbury." George and Jeff lofted the whimsical idea of calling the group The Trembling Wilburys. Dylan suggested altering that to The Traveling Wilburys. Amused, they decided to create a faux biography. They imagined being half-brothers—all sons of the ne'er-do-well Charles Truscott Wilbury. ("Some said Daddy was a cad and a bounder," one son wrote, "but I remember him as a Baptist minister.") Roy Orbison assumed the moniker of "Lefty" Wilbury. George became "Nelson," Bob Dylan "Lucky," Jeff Lynne "Otis," and Tom Petty "Charles T. Wilbury, Jr."[12]

In the spirit of collaboration, all of the songs were considered the creation of everyone in the band, but the main writer of each was not too difficult to decipher. One of Harrison's songs led off the second side of the vinyl LP. Whatever estrangement from God he felt when he wrote "Fish on the Sand" had been reconciled by the time he wrote "Heading for the Light." The lyrics do speak of being "lost in the night" and "close to the edge, hanging by my fingernails," but they characterize that phase as in the process of passing. Now, "I see the sun ahead." Now, "There's nothing in the way to stop me / Heading for the light."

As he neared the end of another decade, Harrison was secure in his accomplishments, his creativity, and his faith.

13

Raindrop on a Lotus Leaf

The Traveling Wilburys, Vol. 1 quickly went double platinum (two million copies shipped) and invigorated the careers of all five members. However, in the midst of a renewal of George's confidence and spirit came a blunt reminder of the fragility of human existence. On December 6, 1988, at just fifty-two years of age, Roy Orbison died suddenly of a heart attack. The Wilburys were scheduled to film a promotional video for "End of the Line" four days later. To include and honor him, the others placed his guitar on an empty rocking chair while they performed.

The year 1989 saw the tumultuous collapse of Communism in Eastern Europe. One of the countries most devastated was Romania, which for decades had suffered under the dictatorship of Nicolae Ceausescu. In the near anarchy that prevailed as 1990 began, approximately one hundred thousand orphans were left to suffer. When Olivia Harrison learned of their plight, their story struck a resonant chord. As the result of what she described as a "gradual assault" on her conscience, she went to Romania to see for herself. What she found overwhelmed her. She appealed to the other Beatles wives—Yoko Ono, Linda McCartney, and Barbara Bach—for help. Aided by Elton John, the four women founded the Romanian Angel Appeal, which raised money for medical aid and supplies and such everyday necessities as sanitation, plumbing, toilets, and washing machines. George agreed to help by producing a benefit album featuring the talents of a number of major names in popular music. He spent April and May with the remaining Traveling Wilburys recording their second album. One of the songs was "Nobody's Child," a Hank Snow classic from the 1940s that George had once recorded with the Beatles in Hamburg. He persuaded the other Wilburys to donate it as the title song of a benefit album to aid the orphans. Following their lead, Elton John, Stevie Wonder, The Bee Gees, Guns 'N' Roses, Van Morrison, Duane Eddy, and Paul Simon all contributed songs to *Nobody's Child: Romanian Angel Appeal.*[1]

On March 20, 1991, Eric Clapton received the telephone call that is every parent's worst nightmare—news of the death of his child. Conor, his four-year-old son by an affair with an Italian model, had been in the company of a housekeeper in the fifty-third-floor apartment belonging to his mother. After cleaning a window, the housekeeper had left the slats ajar to dry. The curious boy slipped out through them onto a ledge, lost his balance, and plummeted to the roof of an adjacent building— a forty-nine-story fall.

Clapton spent several months trying to come to grips with the tragedy. He attended personal therapy sessions and Alcoholics Anonymous meetings. He buried himself in work on the soundtrack for the movie *Rush.* He wrote several songs about his son as an emotional catharsis, most notably "Tears in Heaven." He longed to go on tour as an outlet, but dreaded being the front man while knowing that everyone in the audience would be thinking of his recent heartbreak.

Then it occurred to him that wherever he had traveled in the last decade, he often had to field the question of whether his friend George Harrison would ever return to performing live. To take his mind off his own wretchedness, and perhaps as some contrition for stealing Pattie away, Eric implored George to join him on a tour of Japan. He would organize and direct the backup band, leaving Harrison to star. All George had to do was choose and perform the songs he wanted to play. George, who hadn't toured since the traumatic "Dark Hoarse" tour of 1974, was not easily persuaded. Once he did agree, he vacillated. Finally he came around, and the band gathered for a month of rehearsals, flying to Japan for a twelve-date tour in December 1991.

The arrangement worked. Clapton could lose himself in the creation of the music, and Harrison could enjoy being part of a band without the onerous duties of being a bandleader. He was not suited for the role in any case. According to keyboardist Chuck Leavell, who accompanied him on the Japan tour, George was never comfortable being in command, telling fellow musicians what or how to play. He was too considerate of everyone's feelings. "He would say things like, 'Do you think we should try this song?' or, 'That one isn't really worth doing, is it?' He would never say, 'I want you to play this part,' or, 'Do it like this,' which was somewhat endearing, because it made you feel more involved." Regarding Harrison's kind-hearted attitude toward those around him, Leavell remarked: "During the course of the tour he was always calling up after the show and saying, 'We've got a bit of food—would you like to come and share it with me?' . . . It was all very genuine. . . . He has that kind of personality where there is nothing to hide and he is very open and honest, which can be a refreshing thing in this business."[2]

Al Aronowitz, the journalist who had introduced Bob Dylan to George and knew George well afterward, once observed: "Part of George's charm is that he always feels so inadequate to repay the world for what the world has given him. . . . Acts of kindness have become an art with him." Harrison's sister, Louise, also spoke of George's random and anonymous acts of kindness—paying the hospital bills for people, for example—not because he wanted any acknowledgement or credit, but simply because he thought kind acts ought to be done.[3]

The 1991 tour of Japan was lucrative as well as creatively rewarding and could easily have been continued in other countries, but Harrison was content to let it end there. He had overcome his anxiety about performing in the wake of the dreadful tour of 1974, and he even had the opportunity to bring Dhani on stage to join him in the final concert in Tokyo.

The experience left him less reluctant to take part in concerts afterward. In September, while agonizing about the tour of Japan, he had reconciled with the Maharishi Mahesh Yogi. He flew to the guru's headquarters in Holland in the company of Deepak Chopra. Presenting the Maharishi with a single rose, he offered his sincere apology for the way the Beatles had behaved at Rishikesh—"We were very young." The Maharishi was magnanimous, saying that in his mind the Beatles were angels. "It doesn't matter what John said or did, I could never be upset with angels." Chopra said that, upon being relieved of the "karmic baggage," George broke into tears.

The Maharishi was in the midst of launching the Natural Law Party, a political arm of his organization, in a number of nations. The party's idealistic platform advocated a spiritual lifestyle and the greater use of meditation. On April 6, 1992, perhaps hoping to see the sixties' spirit reignited, George took the stage at Albert Hall to raise funds and generate publicity for the party's slate of candidates in the United Kingdom. He gave the new party his wholehearted support: "I will vote for the Natural Law Party because I want a total change and not just a choice between left and right. . . . I believe this party offers the only option to get out of our problems and create the beautiful nation we would all like to have." He headlined a 105-minute performance that closely adhered to the playlist of the Japan concerts and for an encore brought on Ringo, who had been in the audience and accepted George's invitation to come on stage and join him.[4]

Harrison kept busy in the coming months. In June he appeared with Carl Perkins at London's Hard Rock Café. On October 5, he came on for the encore during bluesman Gary Moore's show at Albert Hall. He performed as part of an all-star assemblage in the Bob Dylan Thirtieth Anniversary Concert in October 1992, singing "If Not for You" and "Absolutely Sweet Marie." On December 14, he joined Eddie Van Halen as part of a fund-raiser for the family of Jeff Porcaro, an ex-member of the group Toto.

Regardless of how emphatically he blazed his own trail as George Harrison, he found that he was always identified as an ex-Beatle. No matter that he had been one only for about a decade, and it had now been over two decades since the breakup. The group had reached such unparalleled heights of popularity that he would be forever branded. Beatles fans had never ceased dreaming that one day the surviving members would reunite and write and record more music. Even George's unequivocal declaration failed to dampen their hopes: "As far as I'm concerned, there won't be a Beatles reunion as long as John Lennon remains dead." And now, in the mid-nineties, the twenty-fifth anniversary of the breakup was fast approaching. People in the industry began to speak of some formal recognition of the event—a look back by the remaining Beatles at what it had been like for them. Against that background, George and the former Beatles' assistant Neil Aspinall came up with an intriguing idea. In the years following John's death, Yoko Ono had selectively released bits and pieces of his works in progress. It was common knowledge that she had in her possession demo recordings he had made during his time as a househusband in the late seventies. Harrison and Aspinall approached her in 1993 to ask if any of the trove was salvageable. Perhaps there could be no more Beatles music created without John, but—but what if he could be included? Did he have any work the others could finish for him?[5]

In January 1994, when Paul McCartney came to New York to induct John into the Rock 'n' Roll Hall of Fame as a solo performer, Yoko gave him John's tapes. In February the three ex-Beatles met at Paul's Mill Studio in Sussex to explore what was possible. Paul proposed that George Martin act as producer, but Harrison insisted on Jeff Lynne, saying that he would bring a more contemporary feel to the music. Four songs offered the best potential—"Free as a Bird," "Real Love," "Grow Old with Me," and "Now and Then."

Setting aside the others until later, they concentrated first on "Free as a Bird," a song Lennon had intended for a musical titled *The Ballad of John and Yoko*. Paul tried to create the right atmosphere by addressing John's absence up front: "When we did 'Sgt. Pepper' we pretended we were other people, so we pretended that John had just rung us up and said, 'I'm going on holiday in Spain. There's this one little song that I like. Finish it up for me. I trust you.'" Submerging their post-

Beatles egos, the three worked to bring out the best in the song. Paul created a restrained bass line and reinforced John's piano work with his own, George added delicate slide guitar licks, and together they wrote lyrics for the bridge. Ringo was elated when he listened to the playback: "It sounds like the bloody Beatles!" Paul would refer to the collaboration as "a joyful experience" and "magic."[6]

They would later perform a similar feat of studio magic on "Real Love." The *Anthology* series consisted of three distinct chronological collections of previously unreleased recordings. Aside from the two "new" Beatles songs, most tracks were simply demos, outtakes, or alternative versions of the band's hits, appealing primarily for the insight they offered into the Beatles' creative process. The fan rapture over what amounted to table scraps proved how enduring the Beatles were as cultural icons. *The Beatles Anthology 1* was released on November 21, 1995, and by mid-December seven million units had been shipped worldwide—almost a million of those in the United States alone during the first week of availability.

Harrison fans had reason to be especially grateful. They could finally hear, from 1958, "In Spite of All the Danger"—the very first recording made by members of the Beatles, a song George wrote with Paul. They could also savor what Paul referred to as "an undiscovered nugget," a long-lost demo of "You Know What to Do," the tune George offered the group after his success with "Don't Bother Me." The demo had turned up unexpectedly when the call went out worldwide to gather all materials identified as Beatles-related for the *Anthology* project. Harrison fans also got to hear the demo of "While My Guitar Gently Weeps," the simple acoustic version George had first played for the others in the band to demonstrate his new song. Paul considered it one of his favorite tracks of the series.

Within the space of one year, all three of *The Beatles Anthology* albums went to the top of the US charts—a phenomenal feat for a band that had been dormant for a quarter of a century. In addition, both singles, "Free as a Bird" and "Real Love," became gold records.

Promoters offered the remaining Beatles $100 million to undertake a ten-concert tour, but more wealth was not the point. None of the three others believed they *were* the Beatles without John Lennon. They even (at George's insistence) decided not to release as a Beatles tune "All for Love"—a song written by Harrison and McCartney and recorded during the *Anthology* sessions.[7]

Both Paul and Ringo took advantage of the immense success of the *Anthology* series to go on to work on solo albums (*Flaming Pie* and *Vertical Man*, respectively). George turned his attention instead to a labor of love. Ravi Shankar planned to create an album that brought the best of India's chanting to the West, and George wanted to produce it.

From the time he first met Shankar in 1966 and began to study the sitar under him, Harrison had maintained a close relationship with the Bengali. He had produced records for him and featured him in the Concert for Bangladesh and the 1974 tour; they attended each other's concerts, they often visited each other's homes, and they met when traveling in cities around the world. Shankar characterized the relationship as multidimensional: "Sometimes I am like a father to him, and sometimes he takes that role with me, while at the same time we are teacher and student, and along with that close friends." George said, "Ravi is probably the person who has influenced my life the most. Maybe he's not aware of it, but I really love Ravi and he's been like a father as well as a spiritual guide. I got involved with Hinduism because Ravi Shankar was a Hindu. And I came to understand what Christ really was through Hinduism."[8]

As Ravi celebrated his seventy-fifth year and Harrison entered what would be the final half-decade of his life, they still shared the deep bonds of religion and music. For George, those were intertwined: "The Vedic system is all about enlightenment, basically, and music is one of the vehicles to gain enlightenment."[9]

They started work on *Chants of India* in early 1996. To cultivate authenticity, they began recording in Madras (modern Chennai)—home of the Madras Music Festival and one of the major centers for music in

South Asia. However, the atmosphere of the studio there seemed too secular for the aura of spirituality they wanted to create. George moved the endeavor to Friar Park. He configured his drawing room as a recording place, positioning the musicians so they could sit on comfortable carpet and gaze through French windows at the gardens outside. To avoid their being distracted by the equipment, he ran cables from the room to the studio on the floor above.

Ravi began the album with invocations to Ganesh, Saraswati, and the universal guru. Following that he featured ancient texts focused on peace, love, ecology, and social harmony. He composed lyrics to two songs himself. Harrison, in addition to producing the sessions, played bass and acoustic guitars, vibraphone, marimba, Autoharp, and glockenspiel.

Whenever Ravi requested, George also added background vocals. His voice comes across especially clearly during a concluding chant, "Om Shanti Shanti Shantihi," which follows the end of the last piece, "Sarvé Shaam." In what was probably no coincidence, he would end his final (posthumous) album, *Brainwashed*, the very same way. With no accompaniment other than that provided by his son Dhani at his side, he honored Shiva and his consort Parvati by chanting the "Namah Parvati" mantra—Shiva being that facet of God symbolizing completion.

George found the work Ravi and his musicians were creating profoundly moving. He approached him after one session with tears in his eyes and hugged him. "Thank you, Ravi, for this music."[10]

Chants of India was released in the United States on May 6, 1997, and in the United Kingdom on September 1.

In July 1997, while outside gardening at Friar Park, Harrison swept his fingers across his neck to wipe away some sweat. He felt a lump he had never noticed before. When he went to a physician to have the lump inspected, several enlarged lymph nodes were discovered. The following month he went to Princess Margaret Hospital in Windsor to have the lumps removed. The incision was a minor one and a spokesman downplayed the surgery. "The operation went without a hitch and we are all confident that it's the end of the matter. George didn't want to take any risks. The procedure was routine and he is now at home and feeling fine."

The procedure may have been routine, but a biopsy of the lumps found cancer. George submitted to two weeks of radiation therapy at the Royal Marsden Hospital in London. When he traveled to America in January to attend the funeral of Carl Perkins, he stopped off at the Mayo Clinic in Rochester, Minnesota, to get an expert opinion. Doctors there concluded that the cancer had been caught and removed in time, and had not spread. After a second checkup in May 1998, a relieved Harrison spoke to the media. He called the incident a "warning." "I got it purely from smoking. . . . It reminds you that anything can happen. Life—there's an old saying—life is like the raindrop on a lotus leaf."[11]

George continued to enjoy life on the lotus leaf while he could. He pursued his passions. He turned up as usual at the Chelsea Flower Show and was a regular at Formula One events around the world. With the thirtieth anniversary of his classic album *All Things Must Pass* nearing, he began to consider how he could mark the occasion and update the work.

On December 23, 1999, a homeless woman broke into George's home on Maui. She laundered her clothes, made telephone calls, and helped herself to pizza from his freezer. George's sister-in-law noticed her and reported the break-in to the police. The woman's only defense was that she felt "a psychic connection" with George. Harrison ultimately declined to press charges, and she was released.[12]

A week later, at 3:20 in the morning of December 30, Olivia woke up from a sound sleep in their Friar Park home. She thought she had heard a chandelier crash to the floor, but as she continued to listen, with mounting uneasiness, she suspected there might be another explanation.

She woke George, who slipped on a jacket and a pair of boots. Going downstairs to investigate, he noticed a cold draft from a shattered window and smelled cigarette smoke. He rushed upstairs again and told Olivia to call for help. She urged him to remain in the bedroom, but his curiosity proved too strong. He returned to the top of the stairs and peered, and after a moment he caught sight of a man emerging from the kitchen. When the man reached the center of the room he glanced up and noticed Harrison. "Who are you?" George called. The intruder screamed back, "You know! Get down here!"

Staring down at the wild-eyed man he had never seen before, George made the worst decision he could have made under the circumstances.

Later he would learn that the thirty-four-year-old intruder, Michael Abram, had a long record of abuse of LSD, cannabis, crack cocaine, and heroin. Diagnosed as "psychotic with paranoid delusions," Abram believed that that he was the archangel Saint Michael, that the Beatles were witches, that they were sending messages to him through their lyrics, and that George in particular was "the alien from Hell"—a sorcerer who was possessing him. Determined to kill Harrison, the deranged Abram had managed to elude all the security measures at Friar Park and dislodge a statue of Saint George and the dragon, which he heaved through a window to gain entry to the house. He had brought with him a knife, and from the statue he had wrested the spear.

Thirty years earlier, filled with terror on the awful flight from Los Angeles to New York to prepare for the Concert for Bangladesh, George had loudly chanted the Hare Krishna mantra until the aircraft landed safely in New York. He was convinced that the mantra had protected him through the crisis. Now he began to chant it again, hoping also that it might confuse and distract the stranger.

Abram later testified that at the moment he spied Harrison at the top of the stairs, he had been having second thoughts about going through with his plan. But when he heard him speaking mysterious words in a strange tongue, he feared it must be a curse. He rushed toward the staircase to kill the witch.

Seeing him come, George tried to retreat to another room but couldn't get the key to turn. He suddenly realized that if the crazed man made it past him nothing would stand between him and Olivia, as well as her mother, who was staying in the house. George made a snap decision to confront the intruder unexpectedly and try to tackle him and wrest the knife away. He whirled and attempted to kick Abram off balance but lost his own balance, and they both tumbled to the floor. Abram ended up on top of him stabbing downward, George trying desperately to deflect the stabs with his hands and arms.

Olivia came to his rescue. She began to strike Abram from behind with a brass poker. It seemed to have no effect on him, except that finally he broke off the attack on George and leaped up to deal with her. Fearing for her safety, George jumped up and tackled Abram from behind. Again they ended up on the floor with Abram on top. Again Abram began to stab downward. George, now exhausted, saw the knife come down to strike his chest. He heard air whoosh from the wound and abruptly tasted blood. He believed he had been fatally stabbed.

Olivia returned to the attack. She grabbed a nearby lamp and clubbed Abram's head again and again. This time it had an effect and Abram toppled over. George now succeeded in wrenching the knife out of the man's hand.

Infuriated, Abram seized the cord from the lamp and began wrapping it around his hands. Olivia, sensing that he meant to strangle her with it, hurled the remnant of the lamp at him and dashed away. He started to pursue her, but then changed his mind and came back toward George, who was still lying on the floor. He struck George on the head again several times and then staggered up to go after Olivia. Dazed and weakened, George turned on his side to watch him and saw the man drop partly to the floor. Just then there were other voices. Uniformed men came dashing up the stairway and secured Abram with handcuffs.

Both George and Olivia were rushed to the Royal Berkshire Hospital. An examination revealed that Harrison had been stabbed five times. One blow, which had punctured and partially deflated a lung, missed his heart by less than an inch.

Allowed to return home on January 1, 2000, George was promptly visited by his friend Eric Idle. Idle insisted on staying at Friar Park for several days to make sure Harrison and his family were all right. Messages of sympathy and good wishes began to arrive from friends all over the world. Tom Petty sent him a fax with just one sentence: "Aren't you glad you married a Mexican girl?"

Though charged with attempted murder on December 31, 1999, Abram began undergoing psychiatric examinations and did not stand trial until the following November. On the second day of his trial, the judge instructed the jury to find Abram not guilty by reason of insanity. Britain's Lunatics Act required such a verdict if the defendant was declared criminally insane at the time of the offense. Remanded to a psychiatric clinic, Abram would be released onto the streets less than two years later.[13]

After recuperating from the assault, Harrison spent much of the year 2000 savoring what Abram had tried to take away from him. He vacationed in the Caribbean, then attended Formula One races in Melbourne, Rio, Montreal, and Indianapolis in March, April, June, and September, respectively. He was now fifty-seven years old, but in spite of all the years, miles, experiences, and scars, he still identified with the apprentice electrician at Blackler's who had daydreamed of life at the top. "Now I understand about 90-year-old people who feel like teenagers because nothing changes. It's just the body that changes. The soul in the body is there at birth and there at death. The only change is the bodily condition."[14]

Still, he was facing the inexorable decline of the body his soul had chosen this time around. Once, when Tom Petty's daughter visited Friar Park and George was showing her around the grounds, he confided to her wistfully, "Oh, Adria, sometimes I just wish I could turn into a light beam and go away."[15]

With the thirtieth anniversary of *All Things Must Pass* fast approaching, Harrison oversaw its remastering to bring the album up to the standards of the digital age. He would rerelease it in January 2001, bolstered by five tracks that included acoustic demos, alternate takes, and one song that had missed the cut in 1970. He reconceived the famous sepia album cover of him surrounded by gnomes in his Friar Park garden by adding color. On the interior CD and booklet covers he reproduced the same photo, only with the sky behind him choked with high-rise buildings, smokestacks, and a highway overpass—his comment on increasing pollution and congestion. He felt dismayed by the direction the world seemed headed at the turn of the millennium—so far afield from the Age of Aquarius that had been the dream of the sixties. In an interview, he said sardonically that he planned to title his next album *The Planet is Doomed, Volume I*. In fact, he *was* working on songs for a new album, but he would title it *Brainwashed* after its most provocative song.

In early 2001, the lacerating truth of one of his favorite lines by Dylan struck home: "He not busy being born is busy dying." It began with a persistent shortness of breath. In March, during another checkup, doctors discovered cancer in his left lung. He immediately flew to the Mayo Clinic for confirmation and entered St. Mary's Hospital in Rochester to undergo a four-hour operation. He remained until April 2. Afterward, he and Olivia flew to Tuscany in Italy, ostensibly for a vacation. But the truth soon came out. The cancer had metastasized and he was actually crossing the border into southern Switzerland for cobalt-radiotherapy treatments on a brain tumor. In July he relocated to his beloved home on Maui, and in August he flew his family on a private jet to India. There, in Benares—ancient Varanasi—he prayed at a temple and took a ritual bath in the sacred waters of the Ganges River.[16]

As he awaited death, George's faith sustained him. Content with all he had achieved in this incarnation, and hopeful that he was about to escape the eternal return and merge with Krishna, he was at peace. Dhani recalled of those final months: "You have to realize that he never sat around moping, 'Oh, I'm ill.' . . . He was never afraid. He was willing to try and get better, but he didn't *care*. He wasn't attached to this world in the way most people would be. He was on to bigger and better things. And he had a real total and utter disinterest in worrying and being stressed. My dad had no fear of dying whatsoever."[17]

When Harrison's strength permitted, he continued work on what was to be his final album. He did so without a heavy heart, and his flippant attitude toward his own mortality came through in a song he cowrote with Dhani for Jools Holland's album, *Small World Big Band*. In October, too weak to play guitar, he sang the lead vocal for "Horse to the Water." Knowing that it was probably his final creative work, he named, as the tune's publishing company, not the customary Harrisongs, but RIP Ltd.[18]

On October 30, George checked into the Staten Island University Hospital for state-of-the-art radiation treatments on his brain tumor. Released on November 10, he remained in the area to be treated as an outpatient. Notified that the end was near, Paul and Ringo visited him at the hospital for several hours on November 12. George left New York on November 17 and flew by Learjet to Los Angeles for chemotherapy and pain management at UCLA Medical Center.

Twelve days later, Olivia and Dhani were at George's bedside in Beverly Hills in the company of Ravi Shankar and his wife, Sukanya, and daughter Anoushka. Also tending him were Harrison's two oldest friends from the Krishna Consciousness movement, Syamasundara Das and Mukunda Goswami. While chanting verses from the Bhagavad Gita, the two devotees sprinkled George's head with drops of water from the Ganges River and placed a garland of tulsi leaves around his neck.

At 1:20 p.m. November 29, 2001, to the soft chanting of the mahamantra, George Harrison passed peacefully away. Late that evening his body was cremated, and with the ashes in their possession Olivia and Dhani immediately left the area by Learjet—bound for the heart of India, it was said, where the ashes would be scattered in the eternal, slow-moving waters of the holy Ganges.[19]

The next day, in the Strawberry Fields area of Central Park, fans gathered together to sing "Here Comes the Sun."

Suggested Listening

"Heading for the Light"
"Any Road"
"Brainwashed"

Epilogue

George Harrison once wrote, "One by one we get awakened by the sound of Krishna's flute. His flute works in many ways."[1] Though his own awakening took place in one night by means of a psychoactive chemical, he was well aware that most people follow more traditional pathways. How a person reaches the goal—yoga, meditation, chanting, an inspiring guru—is immaterial. The goal is to awaken, and George's gentle prodding of those he considered still asleep runs like an undercurrent through his music from the time of his own awakening in the mid-sixties through his final, posthumous album in 2002.

"Are you one of them?" he asks at the end of "Within You without You"—meaning those who hide behind a wall of illusion until it is too late. A year later, to the sound of a mournful guitar, he sadly observes, "I look at you all see the love there's that's sleeping." In "Beware of Darkness," he warns the listener against hopelessness, sadness, maya—"That is not what you are here for." He says straightforwardly in "Awaiting on You All," "The Lord is awaiting on you all to awaken and see." Referring to himself and what he hopes to achieve in "Living in the Material World," he sings, "Got a lot of work to do / Try to get a message through." In "Unconsciousness Rules," he compares the unenlightened life to the oblivion of the dance floor and comments: "Your senses unsatisfied / Take you along on a ride"; "You're living day after day / Where the unconsciousness rules." Just weeks before he died he recorded "Horse to the Water." Its lyrics tell of three troubled individuals he tries to enlighten. The first prefers turning to drugs (or perhaps suicide—"he turned off his nervous system"). The second sufferer opts for the oblivion of whisky. The third, a preacher, is more passionate about condemning "the evils of fornication" than about awakening to discover God in himself.

It saddened Harrison that so few people grasped the truth he saw quite clearly—that we are here to burn out our past karma, to become aware of our divinity, to break free of eternal return. Too few realized how they were squandering their precious opportunity. Like a baby in a crib enchanted by the shiny twirling doodads at arm's length, most people remain too distracted by what they perceive through their five senses to turn their gaze inward and explore what lies within; they keep succumbing again and again to the lures of the material world, mesmerized by its joys, tragedies, pleasures, and fears.

George was still trying to make the point in his final album, *Brainwashed*, released a year after his death through the joint efforts of Dhani and Jeff Lynne. The jaunty first track, "Any Road," talks of "traveling there, traveling here." Yes, he is saying, most of us spend our lives aimlessly meandering, and "If you don't know where you're going / Any road will take you there." But when you decide that you've had enough, once you know where you're going, you need to get onto the right road. So take note, he hinted—"the way out is in."

The title song of the album, "Brainwashed," has a Dylan-like quality, citing a litany of ways people are brainwashed these days in a style reminiscent of "Everybody Must Get Stoned" and "Gotta Serve Somebody." From the days of our youth we are "brainwashed by our leaders," "our teachers," "the school." We're brainwashed constantly, George says, by computers, mobile phones, the military, and ("while you're in a traffic jam") the media. Out of frustration, and hoping to arouse the listener, he repeatedly interrupts the litany with "God God God / Won't you lead us through this mess."

Dhani, who played an indispensable role in finishing the album for his father, had a special fondness for the song: "I just love 'Brainwashed' so much because it's the realest of all the songs. It's true—everyone is being brainwashed by these messages, by taking so much of what we're told and how we live for granted."[2]

To the very end George was saying, Wake up!

It is ironic that, a decade after his death, George Harrison's impact on the world is easy to overlook—ironic because the evidence is all around. Practically every city and town in the Western world has yoga instruction available. The same can be said for meditation. And spread across Christian America are more than 250 Hindu temples, many in the heartland—Idaho, Nebraska, Alabama, Texas—not just in the more predictable places like California and New York. Not to minimize the contribution of Vivekananda, Yogananda, the Maharishi, Prabhupada, and others like them, but let's be honest—would their success have been as far-reaching without the tremendous boost given their efforts through the influence of the Beatles? Yogananda, for instance, spent over thirty years in the West, and the Maharishi a decade, before the Beatles abruptly brought Indian spirituality to everyday awareness. And of the four, Harrison led the way spiritually. He was the first Beatle to embrace chanting and meditation, the first to read *Autobiography of a Yogi* and urge it on the others, the first intrigued by the Maharishi, and the one who first committed to join the guru in Rishikesh—inspiring John and then the others. ("George is a few inches ahead of us," John admitted during their visit to the Maharishi's retreat.)[3] As a result of George's spiritual quest, elements of Eastern culture that likely would have remained exotic diversions in major cities became, with the well-publicized involvement of the Beatles, first "hip" and then acceptable to the mainstream.

In addition, when Harrison was rising to fame the only "foreign" music heard on English-speaking radio consisted of novelty hits such as "Sukiyaki" and "Nel blu dipinto di blu." Today world music is an accepted category wherever music is sold. No doubt much of its success has been driven by the rise of satellite communications and the Internet, but it is indisputable that the process was accelerated by the cultural influence of the Beatles. And George was the Beatle who again led the way for the other three. He was the one captivated by the music of India, the one who made Ravi Shankar famous, and the one responsible for getting the Hare Krishna mantra into the Top Twenty in Britain and making it popular throughout the West. Harrison opened the door that led to the discovery and appreciation, by millions of people, of reggae, the South African "township" sound, salsa, and other music from around the world.

Why is it so easy to overlook Harrison's legacy? The most obvious reason is that he came to fame in the shadow of two remarkably gifted and much more outgoing personalities. John Lennon, with his childhood demons, his prodigious creativity, and his canny grasp of how to exploit his unprecedented fame to advance causes he believed in, cut a swath through the history of his era. Paul McCartney very nearly equaled him. A musical genius and natural showman, Paul has become the most successful songwriter in history and a multifaceted force in modern music—creating everything from rock-and-roll songs, ballads, and film scores to symphonic work, chamber music, two oratorios, and a ballet.

Compared with John and Paul, George was always "the Quiet Beatle." From time to time he stepped into the spotlight—for example, with the thunderous arrival on the charts of *All Things Must Pass* and "My Sweet Lord," or when he produced the Concert for Bangladesh or returned to the public eye with *Cloud Nine* or the Traveling Wilburys. But inevitably, like the Cheshire Cat, he would once again fade away. His motivations for doing what he did were always an enigma to the average fan. He remained a cipher.

People found it difficult to reconcile that someone so "normal" could be associated with matters so alien. John was easily categorized as the crazy artist; perhaps people didn't understand why he was so bent on destroying the goodwill he had built up as a Beatle, but they could categorize him. Paul was the affable extrovert, always in the limelight and perfectly at home there. But George came across as a modest and unpretentious man, someone from the working class, someone who showed up now and then at Formula One events but gave the impression that he preferred being at home working in his garden. George was like Ringo, a good mate.

And yet he would not remain in his box. The occasional article or an interview would reveal some odd new tidbit—the donation of property for a Hindu temple in the United Kingdom, a pilgrimage to an obscure Indian city called Vrindavan, a reunion with the Maharishi and support for his political efforts. George was like a mysterious cloud, drifting in unexpected directions.

Though a cipher, Harrison will always be recalled for his two-pronged legacy—his remarkable music and his deep spirituality.

His songs are as evocative to us now as they were when he first wrote and recorded them. Once the seductive ebb and flow of the rhythm guitar that opens "My Sweet Lord" catches the attention, it takes enormous willpower to focus anywhere else. Who can hear "While My Guitar Gently Weeps" and not sink into a melancholy frame of mind? Who can listen to the delicate "Here Comes the Sun" or the vibrant "Heading for the Light" and not have their spirits lifted? "Something" is as tender a love song as has ever been recorded, considered an instant classic by no less an expert than Frank Sinatra. And the magisterial "All Things Must Pass" (which cries out to be performed by a chorus of a hundred on the same program with "Shenandoah"), leaves even the shallowest listener contemplative.

Aside from his achievements as a recording artist, George is remembered as a spiritual man. Unlike John Lennon, who shared his first, mind-opening LSD trip in 1965, Harrison believed unequivocally in a personal God. Lennon freely used the word "God" in conversation, but for him it was shorthand for a natural, universal background force. Lennon thought of God as an infinite reservoir of energy, likening him to a power station that could be tapped for good or ill.

Harrison instead liked to contemplate God in his human form as Krishna. Sometimes he pictured him as an adult, as a guru or master, but more often than not he preferred to think of him the way he is often portrayed in India—as a baby or as Govinda, the cowherd boy. George enjoyed having the option of relating to God at different times as a teacher, a friend, or a child who evoked his protective instinct.

What seems to be little known, outside Harrison's circle of religious friends, was his veneration of Jesus as well as Krishna. According to Deepak Chopra, who knew George for some fifteen years, Harrison not only was an avid reader of Hindu literature, he also loved to plumb books that presented alternative views of Christianity. Chopra said that he was fascinated by such texts as the Gnostic gospels and the Gospel of Thomas, and that he customarily closed letters to friends with both a Hindu symbol and a Christian cross.[4]

Probably inspired by Yogananda, who repeatedly discusses "Christ-consciousness" in his autobiography, Harrison viewed Jesus as a fully realized incarnation of God who deserved reverence. The poor carpenter from Galilee had come to understand the great secret, burned out his karma, and manifested the deity within himself.

And he was not the only one to do so through the ages. Rama and Buddha, for example, also reached the goal.

As could, presumably, any of us.

In a letter to his mother in 1967, Harrison wrote: "I want to be self-realized. I want to find God. I'm not interested in material things, this world, fame. I'm going for the real goal." Four years later, in early 1971, with *All Things Must Pass* and "My Sweet Lord" atop the charts, George was asked about his future ambitions. "I want to be God-conscious," he replied. "That's really my only ambition, and everything else in life is incidental."[5]

How many of his fellow rock stars would have publicly claimed such a life's goal?

In pursuit of that goal, Harrison found it beneficial to follow a path not commonly traveled in the West—the path of mysticism. While on his 1974 tour of the United States, he told an interviewer: "To me it seems that Western philosophy is very prejudiced because they look upon mysticism as a magical 'something else,' you know? But after everything the greatest Western philosophers have said, to me it all boils down to the fact that they still haven't hit upon what the Eastern people have."[6]

To Harrison, the thinkers of the West were missing the point with their carefully reasoned arguments. Their highly developed mammalian brains lured them further and further along a deceptive path, just as his had done until the day a dose of LSD jolted him out of his sensory straitjacket. From that point forward he grasped the illusory nature of the everyday world around him, and he understood that everything was interrelated.

As he began to meditate regularly and to chant, he came to the conclusion that he was not the physical presence he saw in the mirror—the one the world knew as George Harrison. He was the "I" that inhabited that man, the "I" that could step back and observe that man's problems, hopes, strengths, frailties, ailments, desires, even thoughts.

After he met Ravi Shankar and followed his advice, Harrison began to study what the sages of ancient India had to say about the subject. Those holy men claimed that permeating this teeming ocean of energy we call the universe—and accessible by the trained mind—was the Supreme Deity, fount of all knowledge.

God permeates the great ocean of energy, and the individual soul is like a drop of this ocean. So the "I" that steps back and observes is, more precisely, one tiny part of a "We." Just as a single drop of ocean water contains the same qualities as the entire ocean, each person contains the same qualities God possesses. Everyone, therefore, has the potential to manifest divinity. In fact, doing so is the goal of every person. It can take many incarnations to become aware of the goal, and a great many more to reach it.

Harrison believed that the ancient, esoteric truths ought to be spread around the planet. Such conviction lay behind much of his music, as well as his support of Yogananda's Self-Realization Fellowship and Prabhupada's International Society of Krishna Consciousness—just as he had earlier supported the Maharishi's Spiritual Regeneration Movement. He hoped that a rising tide of people around the world would discover and benefit from Eastern mysticism. He envisioned untold millions of people awakening from their enchantment with maya and grasping the reality that lay just below the surface. In short, he wanted to help every-one achieve the goal he had set for himself in his twenties—becoming self-realized and God-conscious.

And he knew where they could find the beginning of the path lead-ing to the goal, just as he had. "Everyone has within them a drop of that ocean," he once said, "and we have the same qualities as God, just as a drop of the ocean has the same qualities as the entire sea. Every-body's looking for something outside, but it's all right there within ourselves."7

Chronology

1943: On February 24, George Harrison is born at 11:42 p.m. at 12 Arnold Grove, Wavertree, Liverpool.

1945: On March 17, George's future wife, Patricia Boyd, is born.

1948: On May 18, George's second wife, Olivia Trinidad Arias, is born.

1949: George enters Dovedale Primary School. John Lennon is already a student there, two years above him.

1955: In August, George enters the Liverpool Institute, having scored well enough on his final tests to qualify for admission. Another student who takes the same bus each day is James Paul McCartney.

1956: Skiffle player Lonnie Donegan appears at the Empire Theatre in Liverpool. George sees him and develops a fascination for guitars. He learns to play and forms his own skiffle group with his brother Peter.

1957: On July 6, Paul McCartney meets John Lennon and his band, the Quarrymen. George watches the Quarrymen perform on September 7 at the recently opened Cavern Club. On October 18, McCartney performs in public with the Quarrymen for the first time.

1958:   In February or March, Paul introduces George to the Quarrymen. After attending a few engagements as a backup guitarist,
George displaces one of the founders, Eric Griffiths. On July
12, the group records its first record at Percy Philips's studio—
"That'll Be the Day" backed with "In Spite of All the Danger,"
the latter written by McCartney and Harrison. On December
20, the Quarrymen perform at the reception for the marriage of
George's brother Harry.

1959:   On June 19, George ends his formal education by dropping out
of Liverpool Institute.

1960:   In May, the Silver Beatles go on their first tour, to Scotland,
backing a vocalist named Johnny Gentle. In mid-August, the
renamed Beatles travel to Hamburg, Germany, for an engagement at the Indra Club. George is deported on November 21
for being underage. On December 27, the Beatles ("Direct from
Hamburg!") take Litherland Town Hall by storm.

1961:   In April, the Beatles return to Hamburg to play at the Top Ten
Club. On June 22, they back Tony Sheridan in a recording ses-
sion. They also record two of their own numbers, including
"Cry for a Shadow," written by George and John Lennon. On
November 9, Brian Epstein visits the Cavern Club in downtown
Liverpool to see and hear the Beatles. On December 3, Epstein
offers to manage the band.

1962:   On January 1, the Beatles audition for Decca Records. George
sings "The Sheik of Araby" in the failed effort. On April 10,
the band returns to Hamburg and learns that the previous day
Stuart Sutcliffe fell down a flight of stairs and died of a brain
hemorrhage. On June 6, the Beatles visit EMI studios and meet
George Martin. On August 19, Ringo Starr makes his debut

as the Beatles' drummer. On September 4 and 11, Martin records the band playing "Love Me Do," which is released on October 5 and on December 27 peaks in the charts at number seventeen.

1963: On February 22, "Please Please Me" becomes the Beatles' first number one in Britain. In mid-August, while sick in his room in Bournemouth, George writes "Don't Bother Me." From September 16 through October 2, George and his brother Peter vacation in Benton, Illinois, at the home of their sister, Louise. On October 31, the Beatles' return from Sweden causes pandemonium at Heathrow Airport as a huge crowd awaits them in the rain. Two of the travelers inconvenienced are Prime Minister Sir Alec Douglas-Home and American television celebrity Ed Sullivan. On November 4, the Beatles appear before the Queen Mother and Princess Margaret at the Royal Command Performance.

1964: On February 7, the Beatles arrive in New York. Two days later they appear on the *Ed Sullivan Show* to an audience estimated at seventy-four million—four out of ten Americans. Then on March 2, the Beatles begin filming *A Hard Day's Night*. Pattie Boyd, cast for a bit part, mesmerizes George. She accompanies him on trips to Ireland in March and Tahiti in May. On July 6, *A Hard Day's Night* premieres in London. Midway through the Beatles' US tour, on August 28, George meets Bob Dylan, who comes to their hotel room in New York City.

1965: On February 15 and 17, George records two songs for the upcoming second Beatles film, *Help!*—"I Need You" and "You Like Me Too Much." Filming begins in the Bahamas on February 23. In April, George, along with Pattie and John and Cynthia Lennon, first takes LSD. Later in April, George hears sitar music for the first time. During the Beatles' tour of America in August, he first hears records by Ravi Shankar. In October, George uses a sitar to add an exotic flavor to John Lennon's song "Norwegian Wood." On October 26, Harrison receives his MBE medal from Queen Elizabeth II.

1966:   On January 21, George marries Pattie Boyd. In a March 23 interview in London, John Lennon asserts that the Beatles are more popular than Jesus. On June 1, George meets Ravi Shankar, who agrees to teach him to play sitar. During a Beatles world tour, they stop in New Delhi on July 8, where George buys a first-rate instrument. The tour finishes in the United States, where Lennon's comment about Jesus has inflamed Christians. Lennon apologizes, but the Beatles perform in the face of death threats across America. After the final concert in San Francisco, George and John decide that the group will never tour again. George and Pattie fly to Bombay on September 14. The next day, he begins sitar lessons under Ravi Shankar. On October 22, George and Pattie return to England.

1967:   In January, George and John discover Swami Prabhupada's *Krishna Consciousness* album, which offers Hindu chants in praise of Krishna. In February, Pattie begins meditating with a group founded by the Maharishi Mahesh Yogi. George will later follow her lead. On March 15, George and a group of Indian musicians begin recording his song "Within You without You." Though no other Beatle performs on the track, it will be a highlight of *Sgt. Pepper's Lonely Hearts Club Band*. On August 7, in the midst of "the Summer of Love," George visits the Haight-Ashbury district in San Francisco. Repulsed by what he finds, he stops taking LSD. On August 24, the Beatles meet the Maharishi.

1968:   In January, George returns to Bombay to work on the *Wonderwall* album. While there, on January 12, he begins recording "The Inner Light." From February 16 to April 12, George receives advanced training at the Maharishi's Academy of Meditation in Rishikesh, India. After working on *The White Album* all summer, George spends Thanksgiving at Bob Dylan's home in Woodstock, NY.

1969:   On January 10, George walks off the *Let It Be* set, determined to leave the band. He returns only after the others agree to his terms. His home in Esher is raided on March 12 by the London drug squad. On August 22, the Radha Krishna Temple's "Hare Krishna Mantra" is released in the United States on the Apple label. On September 14, George, John, and Yoko Ono interview Swami Prabhupada at Lennon's estate. On October 6, "Something" is released in America, the first and only Harrison composition to appear on the A side of a Beatles' single. On December 2, George (anonymously, as "L'Angelo Mysterioso") makes the first of several appearances with Eric Clapton's new group, Delaney and Bonnie and Friends.

1970:   On January 14, George purchases Friar Park in Henley-on-Thames. In March, he pays for the publication of *KRSNA: The Supreme Personality of the Godhead*. "Govinda," a single by the Radha Krishna Temple, is released in America on March 24. On May 24, George begins work on his solo album *All Things Must Pass*. On July 4, "Something" wins the Ivor Novello award for best song of 1969. George interrupts his recording sessions to visit his mother in Liverpool and is at her bedside when she dies of cancer on July 7. On November 27, *All Things Must Pass* is released in the United States. On the last day of the year, Paul McCartney files a suit to dissolve the Beatles.

1971:   On March 10, the copyright holder to the sixties hit "He's So Fine" publicly alleges that George infringed on its copyright with "My Sweet Lord." In late June, after learning of the dire situation in Bangladesh from Ravi Shankar, George begins organizing a benefit concert. On August 1, the concert takes place in Madison Square Garden—two performances featuring Ravi Shankar, Bob Dylan, Eric Clapton, Ringo Starr, Leon Russell, Billy Preston, and others. The album recorded from the concert is released in America on December 20.

1972:   On January 10, the *Concert for Bangladesh* album is released in Britain. The film of the concert opens in New York on March 23.

1973:   In February, Harrison purchases an English Tudor mansion on a seventeen-acre site in Hertfordshire and donates it to the Radha Krishna Temple. On March 3, the *Concert for Bangladesh* is awarded the Grammy for Album of the Year for 1972. George launches his Material World Charitable Foundation on April 26, to be funded by a portion of his royalties. His album *Living in the Material World* is released in America on May 30 and reaches number one three weeks later. On July 25, irate that the British government will not exempt the charitable *Concert for Bangladesh* album from taxes, George writes Inland Revenue his personal check for one million pounds.

1974:   In February, George visits Vrindavan, a village south of Delhi where Krishna is reputed to have lived. On a visit to Los Angeles he meets an administrative assistant for A&M Records named Olivia Trinidad Arias. He later hires her to work for his own record label, Dark Horse, which he establishes on September 6. On November 2, accompanied by Olivia, he begins a North

America tour in Vancouver, BC. On December 13, in a meeting arranged by the president's son Jack he visits the White House to speak with President Gerald Ford.

1975:   On February 10, Bright Tunes Music begins legal action against George for infringing the copyright to "He's So Fine." He releases his album *Extra Texture (Read All About It)* in America on September 22. On December 26, he appears on Eric Idle's program on BBC 2, *Rutland Weekend Television,* as Pirate Bob singing "The Pirate Song."

1976:   On January 27, after the Beatles' nine-year contract with EMI ends, George signs with his own label, Dark Horse, to be distributed by A&M Records. A judge rules on September 7 that he subconsciously plagiarized "He's So Fine." On November 8, *The Best of George Harrison* is released in the United States, and soon afterward, on November 19, his album *Thirty Three & 1/3* is released in Britain.

1977:   On January 24, George's single "Crackerbox Palace" is released in America, followed by "Dark Horse" on April 4. A London court declares him divorced from Pattie on June 9. He makes a cameo appearance on August 2 on the Monty Python television program *The Rutles*—playing a TV reporter in a spoof of the Beatles. On November 18, the driving force behind the Hare Krishna movement, A. C. Bhaktivedanta Swami Prabhupada, dies at age 81.

1978:   On February 26, George writes "Dark Sweet Lady," inspired by Olivia Trinidad Arias. His first child, Dhani, is born to her on August 1. On September 2, George marries her in a civil ceremony in Henley and they honeymoon in Tunisia. He forms

HandMade Films in September to finance *Monty Python's The Life of Brian*, which has lost its backer. The company will go on to produce such films as *Time Bandits* and *Withnail and I*.

1979: On February 14, the album *George Harrison* is released in America. Eric Clapton marries Pattie on March 27.

1980: George's autobiography, *I Me Mine* (the first and only Beatle autobiography), is published in August in a limited leatherbound edition. The album *Somewhere in England*, scheduled to be released by Warner Bros. on November 2, is postponed when they reject four songs and require that new tunes be written. In the early morning of December 9, George is in bed in Friar Park when his sister, Louise, calls from America with the news that John Lennon has been shot.

1981: On May 11, George releases in the United States "All Those Years Ago"—an affectionate tribute to John Lennon that includes performances by Paul and Ringo. On June 1, *Somewhere in England* is finally released in America with the four replaced songs.

1982: George's album *Gone Troppo* is released in the United States on October 27.

1983: In late March, George, a racing-car buff, attends the Long Beach Grand Prix.

1984: On December 14, George makes a surprise appearance on stage with the rock group Deep Purple, introduced as "Arnold Grove of Liverpool."

1985:   On October 21, George and Ringo perform with one of their boyhood musical heroes in *A Rockabilly Session with Carl Perkins and Friends*.

1986:   On August 29, HandMade Films' *Shanghai Surprise*, starring Sean Penn and Madonna, premieres in New York City. George has a cameo in the film as a nightclub singer.

1987:   "Got My Mind Set on You" is released in Britain on October 12 and four days later in America. *Cloud Nine* is released simultaneously in the United States and United Kingdom on November 2.

1988:   On January 16, "Got My Mind Set on You" reaches number one in America. On January 20, Harrison is inducted, as a member of the Beatles, into the Rock 'n' Roll Hall of Fame. Five days later, "When We Was Fab" is released simultaneously in Britain and America. In May, Harrison meets with an ad hoc group—Roy Orbison, Bob Dylan, Tom Petty, and Jeff Lynne—to write and record "Handle with Care." The five enjoy the collaboration so much that they form a band, the Traveling Wilburys, and create an album together. On June 13, "This Is Love" is released in the United States. *Traveling Wilburys Vol. 1* reaches the market on October 18.

1989:   On July 26, George gives an interview to support a peace march in Hyde Park, London. His single "Cheer Down" is released in America on August 21.

1990:   Olivia visits Romania in May as a volunteer helping Romanian orphans. To support relief efforts, George persuades such luminaries as Ringo Starr, Elton John, Paul Simon, and Stevie

Wonder to record the album *Nobody's Child: Romanian Angel Appeal*, with proceeds donated to the cause.

1991:   On December 1–17, George undertakes a tour of Japan, his first concert tour since the poorly received US tour of 1974. He is supported by Eric Clapton and, for the final concert, by his son, Dhani.

1992:   A double album created from the Japanese tour, *Live in Japan*, is released on July 13 in Britain and in the United States the following day. On October 16, George takes part in an all-star tribute to the music of Bob Dylan, joining Neil Young, Eric Clapton, Willie Nelson, Johnny Cash, Kris Kristofferson, and others.

1993:   On February 20, George is the subject of a tribute show on BBC in honor of his fiftieth birthday. He attends the Spanish Grand Prix in Barcelona on May 9 and the Adelaide Grand Prix on November 7.

1994:   On February 11, George and Ringo join Paul McCartney at Paul's home studio to begin work on John Lennon's song "Free as a Bird," to be released in conjunction with the *Beatles Anthology* project.

1995:   On May 16, the surviving Beatles finish work on "Real Love," another John Lennon demo tape converted into a finished song for the *Beatles Anthology* project. On November 20, the first of three double albums for the project is released.

1996:   In July, George works with Ravi Shankar and a group of Indian musicians on an album titled *Chants of India*.

1997:   On May 6, *Chants of India* is released in the United States. On August 1, George secretly undergoes surgery for throat cancer.

1998:   On January 23, George attends the funeral of his early hero Carl Perkins. On June 29, he announces that the lump removed during his previous surgery was the result of his smoking.

1999:   *Wonderwall*, the film for which Harrison worked on the score in 1968, finally receives its premiere in America on June 26—as part of a sixties film festival in Hollywood. On December 23, a woman breaks into Harrison's home on Maui, eating, making telephone calls, and doing her laundry. One week later, on December 30, a deranged fan, Michael Abram, breaks into Friar Park and assaults both George and Olivia. George suffers several knife wounds and a collapsed lung.

2000:   On April 7, Michael Abram is charged with attempted murder and grievous bodily harm. On June 6, he pleads not guilty. On November 15, the second day of his trial, he is found not guilty by reason of insanity and committed to a mental hospital.

2001:   On March 22, George undergoes four hours of surgery at St. Mary's Hospital in Rochester, Minnesota, to remove a cancer tumor in his left lung. On July 9, he issues a statement from his home in Maui: "I am feeling fine. . . . Please do not worry." On October 1, he records "Horse to the Water," a song he has written with Dhani. On October 30, he enters the Staten Island University Hospital for radiation therapy on a brain tumor. On November 17, he leaves the hospital and goes to Los Angeles to receive chemotherapy at UCLA Medical Center. "Horse to the Water" is released in England on November 19 on the album *Small World Big Band*, by Jools Holland. On November 29,

George Harrison dies peacefully in Beverly Hills surrounded by Olivia, Dhani, Ravi Shankar, and other Hindu friends. He dies while listening to the Hare Krishna mantra and is cremated on the same day, with his ashes to be taken and strewn into the Ganges River.

2002:   On November 18, George's final album, *Brainwashed*, is released.

Notes

Introduction

Epigraph: Ravi Shankar, *Raga Mala: The Autobiography* (New York: Welcome Rain, 1999), 195.
1. Steve Turner, *The Gospel According to the Beatles* (Louisville: Westminster John Knox, 2006), 121.
2. Ibid., 116.

Chapter One

1. George Harrison, *I Me Mine* (New York: Simon and Schuster, 1980), 20–21; Bill Harry, *The George Harrison Encyclopedia* (London: Virgin Books, 2003), 52, 218.
2. Harrison, *I Me Mine*, 28; Joshua M. Greene, *Here Comes the Sun: The Spiritual and Musical Journey of George Harrison* (Hoboken, NJ: John Wiley and Sons, 2006), 3.
3. The Beatles, *The Beatles Anthology* (San Francisco: Chronicle Books, 2000), 25–26; Greene, *Here Comes*, 6–7.
4. Turner, *Gospel*, 39 (see intro., n. 1).
5. Mitchell Glazer, "The George Harrison Interview," *Crawdaddy*, February 1977, 41.
6. Harrison, *I Me Mine*, 22.
7. Ibid., 21; Greene, *Here Comes*, 7.
8. Harrison, *I Me Mine*, 22–23; Greene, *Here Comes*, 8.
9. Philip Norman, *Shout! The Beatles in Their Generation* (New York: Simon and Schuster, Fireside, 1996), 52–53.
10. Harrison, *I Me Mine*, 24–25.
11. Ibid., 23–24; Greene, *Here Comes*, 8.
12. Harrison, *I Me Mine*, 25–26; Norman, *Shout!*, 53.
13. Norman, *Shout!*, 53; Beatles, *Anthology*, 27.
14. Norman, *Shout!*, 53–54; Mark Lewisohn, *The Complete Beatles Chronicle* (London: Hamlyn, Octopus Publishing, 2004), 15–16.
15. Norman, *Shout!*, 55–56.

16. Cynthia Lennon, *A Twist of Lennon* (New York: Avon, 1980), 27; Peter Brown and Steven Gaines, *The Love You Make: An Insider's Story of the Beatles* (New York: Signet, 1984), 30.
17. Beatles, *Anthology*, 31; Harrison, *I Me Mine*, 27, 29.
18. Brown and Gaines, *Love You Make*, 33–34; Ray Coleman, *Lennon* (New York: McGraw-Hill, 1984), 111, 113; Harrison, *I Me Mine*, 29.
19. Lennon, *Twist*, 50; Brown and Gaines, *Love You Make*, 35–36.
20. Greene, *Here Comes*, 6, 15.

Chapter 2

1. Turner, *Gospel*, 70 (see intro., n. 1); Pete Best and Patrick Doncaster, *Beatle! The Pete Best Story* (New York: Dell, 1985), 37, 49.
2. Best and Doncaster, *Beatle*, 36–38.
3. Ibid., 39–42, 46; Coleman, *Lennon*, 130 (see chap. 1, n. 18); Beatles, *Anthology*, 53 (see chap. 1, n. 3).
4. Best and Doncaster, *Beatle*, 50–51.
5. Lewisohn, *Beatles Chronicle*, 22–23 (see chap. 1, n. 14).
6. Best and Doncaster, *Pete Best Story*, 63, 66.
7. Lewisohn, *Beatles Chronicle*, 24; Best and Doncaster, *Beatle*, 70.
8. Best and Doncaster, *Beatle*, 69–73; Lewisohn, *Beatles Chronicle*, 24.
9. Greene, *Here Comes*, 22–23 (see chap. 1, n. 2); Glazer, *Crawdaddy*, 37 (see chap. 1, n. 5).
10. Beatles, *Anthology*, 58, 64 (see chap. 1, n. 3).
11. Lewisohn, *Beatles Chronicle*, 33; Harry, *Encyclopedia*, 53, 141 (see chap. 1, n. 1).
12. Lewisohn, *Beatles Chronicle*, 33–34; Glazer, *Crawdaddy*, 37.
13. Lewisohn, *Beatles Chronicle*, 34–37, 53.
14. Ibid., 56, 70; Harry, *Encyclopedia*, 1.
15. Lewisohn, *Beatles Chronicle*, 58–59; Beatles, *Anthology*, 72.
16. Lewisohn, *Beatles Chronicle*, 88–89, 99–100.
17. Harrison, *I Me Mine*, 84 (see chap. 1, n. 1); William J. Dowlding, *Beatlesongs* (New York: Simon and Schuster, Fireside, 1989), 50.
18. Lewisohn, *Beatles Chronicle*, 110, 127–129.
19. Harry, *Encyclopedia*, 28.
20. Pattie Boyd with Penny Junor, *Wonderful Tonight: George Harrison, Eric Clapton, and Me* (New York: Three Rivers Press, 2007), 14–18, 23–25, 40–41, 56, 61, 63, 67; Lennon, *Twist*, 127–8 (see chap. 1, n. 16).

21. Lewisohn, *Beatles Chronicle*, 138–39; Boyd, *Wonderful Tonight*, 71.
22. Turner, *Gospel*, 99–101; Boyd, *Wonderful Tonight*, 73.

Chapter Three

1. Harrison, *I Me Mine*, 47 (see chap. 1, n. 1); Hunter Davies, *The Beatles: The Authorized Biography* (New York: Dell, 1969), 360.
2. Greene, *Here Comes*, 1–2 (see chap. 1, n. 2).
3. Lewisohn, *Beatles Chronicle*, 139–140 (see chap. 1, n. 14); Greene, *Here Comes*, 48.
4. Lewisohn, *Beatles Chronicle*, 181–182.
5. Dowlding, *Beatlesongs*, 114–125 (see chap. 2, n. 17).
6. Pete Shotton and Nicholas Schaffner, *John Lennon in My Life* (Briarcliff Manor, NY: Stein and Day, 1983), 117; Gary Tillery, *The Cynical Idealist: A Spiritual Biography of John Lennon* (Wheaton, IL: Quest, 2009), 3–4.
7. Turner, *Gospel*, 15, 37–38 (see intro., n. 1); Dowlding, *Beatlesongs*, 127.
8. Beatles, *Anthology*, 26 (see chap. 1, n. 3).
9. Turner, *Gospel*, 37, 41.
10. Coleman, *Lennon*, 312 (see chap. 1, n. 18).
11. Ibid., 316.
12. Lewisohn, *Beatles Chronicle*, 213, 230.
13. Greene, *Here Comes*, 48; Turner, *Gospel*, 34.
14. Marc Shapiro, *Behind Sad Eyes: The Life of George Harrison* (New York: St. Martin's Press, 2002), 74: Coleman, *Lennon*, 317.
15. Turner, *Gospel*, 16.

Chapter Four

1. Turner, *Gospel*, 112–13 (see intro., n. 1); Timothy Leary, Ralph Metzner, and Richard Alpert, *The Psychedelic Experience: A Manual Based on the Tibetan Book of the Dead* (New York: Citadel Press, 1990), 11.
2. Norman, *Shout!*, 244–45 (see chap. 1, n. 9); Brown and Gaines, *Love You Make*, 157–59 (see chap. 1, n. 16); Turner, *Gospel*, 114–17; Boyd, *Wonderful Tonight*, 100–102 (see chap. 2, n. 20); Harry, *Encyclopedia*, 256 (see chap. 1, n. 1).
3. Belmo, *George Harrison: His Words, Wit & Wisdom* (Canada: Belmo Publishing, 2002), 46.
4. Turner, *Gospel*, 116.

5. The Editors of Rolling Stone, *Harrison* (New York: Simon and Schuster, 2002), 145.
6. "The Playboy Interview: Timothy Leary," *Playboy*, September 1966, accessed Nov. 11, 2010, http://www.archive.org/details/playboylearyinte00playrich, 3.
7. Derek Taylor, *It Was Twenty Years Ago Today* (New York: Simon and Schuster, Fireside, 1987), 93; Harry, *Encyclopedia*, 256 (see chap. 1, n. 5).
8. R. Gordon Wasson, Albert Hofmann, and Carl A. P. Ruck, *The Road to Eleusis: Unveiling the Secret of the Mysteries* (Berkeley, CA: North Atlantic Books, 2008), 27, 29, 38, 42–43, 46–47, 57–58, 159.
9. Turner, *Gospel*, 113–17; Boyd, *Wonderful Tonight*, 102.
10. J. Kordosh, "The George Harrison Interview," *Creem*, January 1988, accessed Nov. 11, 2010, http://beatlesnumber9.com/creem.html.
11. Turner, *Gospel*, 111.
12. Lennon, *Twist*, 155 (see chap. 1, n. 16); Jonathan Cott and Christine Doudna, eds., *The Ballad of John and Yoko* (Garden City, NY: Doubleday, 1982), 68.
13. A. C. Bhaktivedanta, Swami Prabhupada, *KRSNA: The Supreme Personality of Godhead*, vol. 1 (Mumbai: Bhaktivedanta Book Trust, 1972), intro. note.
14. Turner, *Gospel*, 118.
15. Turner, *Gospel*, 130–31; Boyd, *Wonderful Tonight*, 104–105; Greene, *Here Comes*, 82–83 (see chap. 1, n. 2), 157; Taylor, *Twenty Years Ago*, 122–23; Beatles, *Anthology*, 259 (see chap. 1, n. 3).
16. Beatles, *Anthology*, 259; Turner, *Gospel*, 131.
17. Taylor, *Twenty Years Ago*, 126–27.

Chapter Five

1. Turner, *Gospel*, 136 (see intro., n. 1); Dowlding, *Beatlesongs*, 137 (see chap. 2, n. 17).
2. Ravi Shankar, *Raga Mala*, 190 (see intro., epigraph).
3. Belmo, *Wit & Wisdom*, 24 (see chap. 4, n. 3); Mia Farrow, *What Falls Away* (New York: Doubleday, Nan A. Talese, 1997), 138.
4. Shankar, *Raga Mala*, 195 (see intro., epigraph).
5. Paramahansa Yogananda, *Autobiography of a Yogi* (Los Angeles: Self Realization Fellowship, 2000), 478; Swami Vivekananda, *Raja Yoga* (Kolkata: Advaita Ashrama, 2009), 87.

6. Boyd, *Wonderful Tonight*, 88, 160 (see chap. 2, n. 20); Shankar, *Raga Mala*, 222.

7. Beatles Interviews Database, "Sgt. Pepper Launch Party 5/19/67," accessed Nov. 12, 2010, http://www.beatlesinterviews.org/db1967.0519.beatles.html; Turner, Gospel, 10.

8. Shankar, *Raga Mala*, 195.

9. Turner, *Gospel*, 141; Bhaktivedanta Book Trust, *Search for Liberation* (Los Angeles: Bhaktivedanta Book Trust, 1981), v; Bhaktivedanta Book Trust, *Chant and Be Happy: the Power of Mantra Meditation* (Bhaktivedanta Book Trust, 1982, Internet edition accessed July 9, 2010, http://harekrishna.com /col/books/YM/cbh/ch1.html), 6.

10. Turner, *Gospel*, 129; Dowlding, *Beatlesongs*, 174–75 (see chap. 2, n. 17).

11. Dowlding, *Beatlesongs*, 156; Paul Mason, *The Maharishi* (Rockport, MA: Element, 1994), 106.

12. Boyd, *Wonderful Tonight*, 96, 106–108; Lennon, *Twist*, 164 (see chap. 1, n. 20).

13. Mason, *The Maharishi*, 120–24.

14. Turner, *Gospel*, 145.

15. Dowlding, *Beatlesongs*, 201–202.

16. Mason, *The Maharishi*, 74–75, 96–97, 130–34; Harold H. Bloomfield, Michael Peter Cain, and Dennis T. Jaffe, *TM*: Discovering Inner Energy and Overcoming Stress* (New York: Delacorte, 1975), 183–84; Beatles, *Anthology*, 281 (see chap. 1, n. 3).

17. Mason, *The Maharishi*, 138–39; Boyd, *Wonderful Tonight*, 116, 119; Farrow, *What Falls Away*, 140–41.

Chapter Six

1. Steve Turner, *A Hard Day's Write: The Stories behind Every Beatles Song*, (Dubai: Carlton Books, 2005), 129.

2. Boyd, *Wonderful Tonight*, 122–23 (see chap. 2, n. 20).

3. Norman, *Shout!*, 340 (see chap. 1, n. 9); Lewisohn, *Beatles Chronicle*, 283–304 (see chap. 1, n. 14).

4. Greene, *Here Comes*, 102–104 (see chap. 1, n. 2); Boyd, *Wonderful Tonight*, 160.

5. Greene, *Here Comes*, 106–110.

6. Turner, *Gospel*, 151 (see intro., n. 1); Bhaktivedanta Book Trust, *Search for Liberation*, v–vi, 14, 15, 19, 26, 27, 29 (see chap. 5, n. 9).

7. Georgeharrison.com, "Memories of George Harrison," accessed Nov. 12, 2010, http://board.georgeharrison.com//viewtopic.php?q=board/viewtopic.php&f=7&t=5900&p=122131.

Chapter Seven

1. Klaus K. Klostermaier, *Hinduism: A Short Introduction* (Oxford: Oneworld, 2005), 9, 10, 12–15.

2. Ibid., 16–17; Radhakrishnan, *The Hindu View of Life* (New York: MacMillan, 1973), 18.

3. Radhakrishnan, *Hindu View*, 36.

4. Ibid., 32–33.

5. Bhaktivedanta, *KRSNA*, intro. (see chap. 4, n. 13); Belmo, *Wit & Wisdom*, 32 (see chap. 4, n. 3).

6. A. C. Bhaktivedanta, Swami Prabhupada, *Bhagavad-Gita as It Is* (Los Angeles: Bhaktivedanta Book Trust, 2006), viii–xi; Shankar, *Raga Mala*, 196 (see intro., epigraph).

7. Robert D. Richardson, Jr., *Emerson: The Mind on Fire* (Berkeley, CA: University of California Press, 1995), 114, 115; Henry David Thoreau, *Walden or, Life in the Woods (and On the Duty of Civil Disobedience)* (New York: Signet, 1980), 198.

8. Greene, *Here Comes*, 287, n. 84 (see chap. 1, n. 2); C. F. Andrews, *Mahatma Gandhi's Ideas: Including Selections from his Writings* (New York: MacMillan, 1930), 73.

9. Greene, *Here Comes*, 178, 200; Bhaktivedanta Book Trust, *Chant and Be Happy*, 20 (see chap. 5, n. 9).

10. Bhaktivedanta, *Gita as It Is*, 201, 203; Yogananda, *Autobiography*, 297 (see chap. 5, n. 5).

11. Yogananda, *Autobiography*, 300, 303, 305–313.

12. Ibid., 341–45.

Chapter Eight

1. Vic Garbarini and Brian Cullman, with Barbara Graustark, *Strawberry Fields Forever: John Lennon Remembered* (New York: Bantam, Delilah, 1980), 101.

2. Lewisohn, *Beatles Chronicle*, 307–309 (see chap. 1, n. 14); Greene, *Here Comes*, 112, 115 (see chap. 1, n. 2).

3. Greene, *Here Comes*, 178.

4. Bhaktivedanta Book Trust, *Chant and Be Happy*, 11 (see chap. 5, n. 9).

5. Harrison, *I Me Mine*, 176 (see chap. 1, n. 1); Editors of Rolling Stone, *Harrison*, 233 (see chap. 4, n. 5).

6. Harrison, *I Me Mine*, 200.

7. Ibid., 179.

8. Greene, *Here Comes*, 182.

9. Boyd, *Wonderful Tonight*, 148, 160–61 (see chap. 2, n. 20); Greene, *Here Comes*, 173.

10. Harry, *Encyclopedia*, 321 (see chap. 1, n. 1).

11. Chris O'Dell, with Katherine Ketcham, *Miss O'Dell: My Hard Days and Long Nights with The Beatles, The Stones, Bob Dylan, Eric Clapton, and the Women They Loved* (New York: Simon and Schuster, Touchstone, 2009), 139–40; Brown and Gaines, *Love You Make*, 350 (see chap. 1, n. 16).

12. Boyd, *Wonderful Tonight*, 79, 80, 96, 114, 138–39, 168.

13. Ibid., 154–56, 171–74.

14. Ibid., 179–80.

15. O'Dell, *Miss O'Dell*, 256–64.

16. Boyd, *Wonderful Tonight*, 182, 184; Greene, *Here Comes*, 206–208.

Chapter Nine

1. James Wynbrandt, *A Brief History of Pakistan* (New York: Facts on File, 2009), 186–89, 199–201.

2. Shankar, *Raga Mala*, 217–20 (see intro., epigraph).

3. Bhaktivedanta Book Trust, *Chant and Be Happy*, 5 (see chap. 5, n. 9); Shankar, *Raga Mala*, 220; Greene, *Here Comes*, 186–93(see chap. 1, n. 2); Michael Schumacher, *Crossroads: The Life and Music of Eric Clapton* (New York: Hyperion, 1995), 164–65; Editors of Rolling Stone, *Harrison*, 122–23 (see chap. 4, n. 5).

4. Greene, *Here Comes*, 193–94; Harry, *Encyclopedia*, 74 (see chap. 1, n. 1).

Chapter Ten

1. Greene, *Here Comes*, 183–84 (see chap. 1, n. 2).

2. Harrison, *I Me Mine*, 70 (see chap. 1, n. 1); Greene, *Here Comes*, 172; Harry, *Encyclopedia*, 224 (see chap. 1, n. 1).
3. Bhaktivedanta Book Trust, *Chant and Be Happy*, 3, 7 (see chap. 5, n. 9); Greene, *Here Comes*, 173, 202–203.
4. Bhaktivedanta, *KRSNA*, viii–ix (see chap. 4, n. 13).
5. Belmo, *Wit & Wisdom*, 53 (see chap. 4, n. 3).
6. Schumacher, *Crossroads*, 178 (see chap. 9, n. 3).
7. Vivekananda, *Raja Yoga*, iv (see chap. 5, n. 5); Greene, *Here Comes*, 6.
8. Bhaktivedanta Book Trust, *Chant and Be Happy*, 8; Greene, *Here Comes*, 243; Bhaktivedanta, *Gita As It Is*, 263 (see chap. 7, n. 6).
9. Greene, *Here Comes*, 179–80; Beatles, *Anthology*, 267 (see chap. 1, n. 3).
10. Bhaktivedanta Book Trust, *Chant and Be Happy*, 4, 6.
11. Harrison, *I Me Mine*, 200.
12. Bhaktivedanta, *KRSNA*, viii–ix.
13. Bhaktivedanta Book Trust, *Chant and Be Happy*, 20; Harrison, *I Me Mine*, 203.

Chapter Eleven

1. Boyd, *Wonderful Tonight*, 161 (see chap. 2, n. 20).
2. Bhaktivedanta Book Trust, *Chant and Be Happy*, 18 (see chap. 5, n. 9).
3. Harry, *Encyclopedia*, 253, 391 (see chap. 1, n. 1).
4. Bhaktivedanta Book Trust, *Chant and Be Happy*, 5.
5. Harrison, *I Me Mine*, 296–97 (see chap. 1, n. 1).
6. Greene, *Here Comes*, 235 (see chap. 1, n. 2).
7. Ibid., 213–15; Shapiro, *Behind Sad Eyes*, 131–32 (see chap. 3, n. 14).
8. Harrison, *I Me Mine*, 69; Shapiro, *Behind Sad Eyes*, 133.
9. Harry, *Encyclopedia*, 371–72.
10. Dale C. Allison, Jr. *The Love There That's Sleeping: The Art and Spirituality of George Harrison* (New York: Continuum, 2006), 7; Harry, *Encyclopedia*, 78, 223.
11. Shapiro, *Behind Sad Eyes*, 138; Harry, *Encyclopedia*, 397.
12. Harrison, *I Me Mine*, 326; Greene, *Here Comes*, 225, 228.
13. Harry, *Encyclopedia*, 48–49, 70, 72, 81, 84; Editors of Rolling Stone, *Harrison*, 156 (see chap. 4, n. 5); Beatles, *Anthology*, 83 (see chap. 1, n. 3).

14. Greene, *Here Comes*, 212.

15. Ibid., 230; Harry, *Encyclopedia*, 79, 81, 272–73; Elliot J. Huntley, *Mystical One: George Harrison: After the Break-Up of the Beatles* (Toronto: Guernica, 2006), 154–55.

16. Belmo, *Wit & Wisdom*, 56 (see chap. 4, n. 3); Henley *Standard*, "Beatle George Rejected Film Role," accessed on October 25, 2010, http://www.henleystandard.co.uk/news/news.php?id=669868, 26 Oct 2009.

17. Harry, *Encyclopedia*, 217, 223; Shankar, *Raga Mala*, 229 (see intro., epigraph).

18. Shapiro, *Behind Sad Eyes*, 152.

Chapter Twelve

1. Harrison, *I Me Mine*, 39–41 (see chap. 1, n. 1); Shapiro, *Behind Sad Eyes*, 154, 155 (see chap. 3, n. 14).

2. Huntley, *Mystical One*, 176 (see chap.11, n. 15); Mark Rowland, "The Quiet Wilbury," *Musician*, March 1990, 36; Shapiro, *Behind Sad Eyes*, 7; Greene, *Here Comes*, 233 (see chap. 1, n. 2).

3. Harry, *Encyclopedia*, 17–18, 85–86 (see chap. 1, n. 1).

4. Bhaktivedanta Book Trust, *Chant and Be Happy*, 20 (see chap. 5, n. 9).

5. Paul Theroux, "George Harrison's Haven," *Architectural Digest*, August 2007, accessed July 30, 2010, http://www.architecturaldigest.com/homes/features/2007/08/harrison_article_082007.

6. Harry, *Encyclopedia*, 192.

7. Shapiro, *Behind Sad Eyes*, 156, 159; Belmo, *Wit & Wisdom*, 57 (see chap. 4, n. 3).

8. Harry, *Encyclopedia*, 88–90.

9. Ibid., 114, 294–95, 332–38.

10. Huntley, *Mystical One*, 206–212; Harry, *Encyclopedia*, 131; Belmo, *Wit & Wisdom*, 54.

11. Huntley, *Mystical One*, 214–15.

12. Ibid., 219–20; Editors of Rolling Stone, *Harrison*, 157 (see chap. 4, n. 5); Ellis Amburn, *Dark Star: The Roy Orbison Story* (New York: Knightsbridge, 1991), 218–19; Squidoo, "The Traveling Wilburys," accessed Nov. 9, 2010, http://www.squidoo.com/thetravelingwilburys.

Notes

Chapter Thirteen

1. Huntley, *Mystical One*, 226–28 (see chap. 11, n. 15).
2. Schumacher, *Crossroads*, 296–301 (see chap. 9, n. 3); Huntley, *Mystical One*, 233–35, 239.
3. Greene, *Here Comes*, 180 (see chap. 1, n. 2).
4. Turner, *Gospel*, 178–79 (see intro., n. 1); Huntley, *Mystical One*, 240–41.
5. Huntley, *Mystical One*, 242–43, 249–250; *New York Times*, "No 3-Beatle Reunion, Harrison Says," accessed Oct. 27, 2010, http://www.nytimes.com/keyword/ringo/3.
6. Huntley, *Mystical One*, 252, 254, 255.
7. Ibid., 262–68.
8. Shankar, *Raga Mala*, 230 (see intro., epigraph); Harry, *Encyclopedia*, 321 (see chap. 1, n. 1).
9. Harry, *Encyclopedia*, 321.
10. Shankar, *Raga Mala*, 305, 308.
11. Harry, *Encyclopedia*, 45–46.
12. Ibid., 113, 115, 117.
13. Ibid., 6–9, 115; Editors of Rolling Stone, *Harrison*, 49, 225 (see chap. 4, n. 5).
14. Belmo, *Wit & Wisdom*, 68 (see chap. 4, n. 3).
15. Editors of Rolling Stone, *Harrison*, 225.
16. Harry, *Encyclopedia*, 116–18, 322; Shapiro, *Behind Sad Eyes*, 194–95 (see chap. 3, n. 14).
17. Christopher Scapelliti, "Handle With Care," *Guitar World*, January 2003, 112.
18. Allison, *Love That's Sleeping*, 93, 145 (see chap. 11, n. 10); Harry, *Encyclopedia*, 119.
19. Harry, *Encyclopedia*, 119, 322; Bhaktivedanta Memorial Library, "The Last Minutes of George Harrison," accessed Dec. 5, 2010, http://bvml.org/contemporary/tlmogh.html.

Epilogue

1. Shankar, *Raga Mala*, 195 (see intro., epigraph).
2. Scapelliti, "Handle with Care," 58 (see chap. 13, n. 17).
3. Beatles, *Anthology*, 281 (see chap. 1, note 3).

4. Steve Waldman, "Deepak Chopra on his Friend George Harrison," Belief-net.com, accessed Nov. 23, 2010, www.beliefnet.com/story/94/story_9434.html.
5. Scapelliti, "Handle with Care," 114; Greene, *Here Comes*, 184 (see chap. 1, n. 2).
6. Turner, *Gospel*, 10 (see intro., n. 1).
7. Belmo, *Wit & Wisdom*, 36 (see chap. 4, n. 3).

Bibliography

Allison, Dale C., Jr. *The Love There That's Sleeping: The Art and Spirituality of George Harrison*. New York: Continuum, 2006.

Amburn, Ellis. *Dark Star: The Roy Orbison Story*. New York: Knightsbridge, 1991.

Andrews, C. F. *Mahatma Gandhi's Ideas: Including Selections from his Writings*. New York: MacMillan, 1930.

Beatles, The. *The Beatles Anthology*. San Francisco: Chronicle Books, 2000.

———. *The Beatles Lyrics*. Compilation. London: Futura, 1983.

Beatles Interviews Database. "Sgt. Pepper Launch Party 5/19/67." Accessed Nov. 12, 2010. http://www.beatlesinterviews.org/db1967.0519.beatles.html.

Belmo. *George Harrison: His Words, Wit & Wisdom*. Canada: Belmo Publishing, 2002.

Best, Pete and Patrick Doncaster. *Beatle! The Pete Best Story*. New York: Dell, 1985.

Bhaktivedanta, A. C., Swami Prabhupada. *Bhagavad-Gita As It Is*. Los Angeles: Bhaktivedanta Book Trust, 2006.

———. *KRSNA: The Supreme Personality of Godhead*. Vol. 1. Mumbai: Bhaktivedanta Book Trust, 1972.

Bhaktivedanta Book Trust. *Chant and Be Happy: the Power of Mantra Meditation*. Bhaktivedanta Book Trust, 1982. Internet edition accessed July 9, 2010. http://harekrishna.com/col/books/YM/cbh/ch1.html.

―――. *Search for Liberation*. Los Angeles: Bhaktivedanta Book Trust, 1981. (Featuring a conversation between A. C. Bhaktivedanta, Swami Prabhupada, and John Lennon.)

Bhaktivedanta Memorial Library. "The Last Minutes of George Harrison." Accessed Dec. 5, 2010. http://bvml.org/contemporary/tlmogh .html.

Bloomfield, Harold H., Michael Peter Cain, and Dennis T. Jaffe. *TM*: Discovering Inner Energy and Overcoming Stress*. New York: Delacorte, 1975.

Boyd, Pattie with Penny Junor. *Wonderful Tonight: George Harrison, Eric Clapton, and Me*. New York: Three Rivers Press, 2007.

Brown, Peter and Steven Gaines. *The Love You Make: An Insider's Story of the Beatles*. New York: Signet, 1984.

Coleman, Ray. *Lennon*. New York: McGraw-Hill, 1984.

Cott, Jonathan, and Christine Doudna, eds. *The Ballad of John and Yoko*. Garden City, NY: Doubleday, 1982.

Davies, Hunter. *The Beatles: The Authorized Biography*. New York: Dell, 1969.

Dowlding, William J. *Beatlesongs*. New York: Simon and Schuster, Fireside, 1989.

Farrow, Mia. *What Falls Away*. New York: Doubleday, Nan A. Talese, 1997.

Garbarini, Vic, and Brian Cullman, with Barbara Graustark. *Strawberry Fields Forever: John Lennon Remembered*. New York: Bantam, Delilah, 1980.

GeorgeHarrison.com. "Memories of George Harrison." Accessed Nov. 12, 2010. http://board.georgeharrison.com//viewtopic.php?q=board /viewtopic.php&f=7&t=5900&p=122131.

Glazer, Mitchell. "The George Harrison Interview." *Crawdaddy*, February 1977.

Greene, Joshua M. *Here Comes the Sun: The Spiritual and Musical Journey of George Harrison*. Hoboken, NJ: John Wiley and Sons, 2006.

Harrison, George. *I Me Mine*. New York: Simon and Schuster, 1980.

Harry, Bill. *The George Harrison Encyclopedia*. London: Virgin Books, 2003.

Henley *Standard*. "Beatle George Rejected Film Role." Accessed Oct. 25, 2010. http://www.henleystandard.co.uk/news/news.php?id=669868, 26 Oct 2009.

Huntley, Elliot J. *Mystical One: George Harrison: After the Break-Up of the Beatles*. Toronto: Guernica, 2006.

Klostermaier, Klaus K. *Hinduism: A Short Introduction*. Oxford: Oneworld, 2005.

Kordosh, J. "The George Harrison Interview." *Creem*, January 1988. Accessed Nov. 11, 2010. http://beatlesnumber9.com/creem.html.

Leary, Timothy, Ralph Metzner, and Richard Alpert. *The Psychedelic Experience: A Manual Based on the Tibetan Book of the Dead*. New York: Citadel Press, 1990.

Lennon, Cynthia. *A Twist of Lennon*. New York: Avon Books, 1980.

Lewisohn, Mark. *The Complete Beatles Chronicle*. London: Hamlyn, Octopus Publishing, 2004.

Mason, Paul. *The Maharishi*. Rockport, MA: Element, 1994.

New York Times. "No 3-Beatle Reunion, Harrison Says." Accessed Oct. 27, 2010.http://www.nytimes.com/keyword/ringo/3.

Norman, Philip. *Shout! The Beatles in Their Generation*. New York: Simon and Schuster, Fireside, 1996.

O'Dell, Chris, with Katherine Ketcham. *Miss O'Dell: My Hard Days and Long Nights with The Beatles, The Stones, Bob Dylan, Eric Clapton, and the Women They Loved*. New York: Simon and Schuster, Touchstone, 2009.

Playboy. "The Playboy Interview: Timothy Leary." September 1966. Accessed Nov 11, 2010. http://www.archive.org/details /playboylearyinte00playrich.

Radhakrishnan. *The Hindu View of Life*. New York: MacMillan, 1973.

Richardson, Jr., Robert D. *Emerson: The Mind on Fire*. Berkeley, CA: University of California Press, 1995.

Rolling Stone, The Editors of. *Harrison*. New York: Simon and Schuster, 2002.

Rowland, Mark. "The Quiet Wilbury." *Musician*, March 1990.

Scapelliti, Christopher. "Handle With Care." *Guitar World*, January 2003.

Schumacher, Michael. *Crossroads: The Life and Music of Eric Clapton*. New York: Hyperion, 1995.

Shankar, Ravi. *Raga Mala: The Autobiography of Ravi Shankar*. New York: Welcome Rain, 1999.

Shapiro, Marc. *Behind Sad Eyes: The Life of George Harrison*. New York: St. Martin's Press, 2002.

Shotton, Pete and Nicholas Schaffner. *John Lennon in My Life*. Briarcliff Manor, NY: Stein and Day, 1983.

Squidoo. "The Traveling Wilburys." Accessed Nov. 9, 2010. http://www .squidoo.com/thetravelingwilburys.

Taylor, Derek. *It Was Twenty Years Ago Today*. New York: Simon and Schuster, Fireside, 1987.

Theroux, Paul. "George Harrison's Haven." *Architectural Digest*, August 2007. Accessed July 30, 2010. http://www.architecturaldigest.com/ homes/features/2007/08/ harrison_article_082007.

Thoreau, Henry David. *Walden or, Life in the Woods (and On the Duty of Civil Disobedience)*. New York: Signet, 1980.

Tillery, Gary. *The Cynical Idealist: A Spiritual Biography of John Lennon*. Wheaton, IL: Quest, 2009.

Turner, Steve. *The Gospel According to the Beatles*. Louisville: Westminster John Knox, 2006.

———. *A Hard Day's Write: The Stories Behind Every Beatles Song*. Dubai: Carlton Books, 2005.

Vivekananda, Swami. *Raja Yoga*. Kolkata: Advaita Ashrama, 2009.

Waldman, Steve. "Deepak Chopra on his Friend George Harrison." Beliefnet.com, no date. Accessed Nov. 23, 2010. www.beliefnet.com /story/94/story_9434.html.

Wasson, R. Gordon, Albert Hofmann, and Carl A. P. Ruck. *The Road to Eleusis: Unveiling the Secret of the Mysteries*. Berkeley, CA: North Atlantic Books, 2008.

Wynbrandt, James. *A Brief History of Pakistan*. New York: Facts on File, 2009.

Yogananda, Paramahansa. *Autobiography of a Yogi*. Los Angeles: Self Realization Fellowship, 2000.

Index

About the Author

Gary Tillery was born in Phoenix in 1947. Beginning in 1968, he served in Vietnam with the United States Air Force. When his enlistment was over in 1970, he earned a Bachelor's degree in Latin American Studies from Arizona State University and a Master's degree from the American Graduate School of International Management.

After two decades as a co-owner of an advertising agency in suburban Chicago, Tillery turned to his lifelong passion for literature and art. He published a collection of interrelated short stories set in Vietnam titled *Darkling Plain* and began a series of humorous novels featuring "soft-boiled" detective Jack Savage—the first two titled *Death, Be Not Loud* and *To an Aesthete Dying Young*. Tillery's fascination with John Lennon led him to write *The Cynical Idealist*, in which he constructs a coherent view of Lennon's philosophy—one that was idealistic yet pragmatic.

Tillery is also a professional sculptor, using the traditional mediums of metal and stone to express contemporary ideas. His most prominent work is the sculpture for the Vietnam Memorial in Chicago. He has displayed in galleries from Pennsylvania to New Mexico and appeared in shows as far away as Shanghai. His works are in the private collections of Patricia DuPont and General Tommy Franks, and the National Vietnam Veterans Art Museum in Chicago possesses two pieces in its permanent collection.

Quest Books

encourages open-minded inquiry into
world religions, philosophy, science, and the arts
in order to understand the wisdom of the ages,
respect the unity of all life, and help people explore
individual spiritual self-transformation.

Its publications are generously supported by
The Kern Foundation,
a trust committed to Theosophical education.

Quest Books is the imprint of
the Theosophical Publishing House,
a division of the Theosophical Society in America.
For information about programs, literature,
on-line study, membership benefits, and international centers,
see www.theosophical.org
or call 800-669-1571 or (outside the U.S.) 630-668-1571.

Related Quest Titles

The Cynical Idealist, by Gary Tillery
The Meditative Path, by John Cianciosi
Mother of the Universe, by Lex Hixon
The Other Half of My Soul, compiled by Beatrice Bruteau
The Transcendent Unity of Religions, by Frithjof Schuon
The Wisdom of the Vedas, by J. C. Chatterji
Yoga for Your Spiritual Muscles, by Rachel Schaeffer

To order books or a complete Quest catalog,
call 800-669-9425 or (outside the U.S.) 630-665-0130.

More Praise for Gary Tillery's

Working Class
MYSTIC

"In this often troubled and desensitized world of stone, Gary Tillery's elegantly written account of Harrison's musical and spiritual life arrives to us as if on the wings of angels."

> —**Anthony Pomes**, advisory board member of the
> John Lennon Center for Music and Technology

"From the early days I noticed George had an inner talent. . . . I actually encouraged him to begin writing again after he seemed blocked by the song-writing success of Lennon and McCartney. I saw how he became the Beatle most stretched by his friends, his philosophy, and his search for meaning—a meaning which he eventually discovered. Gary Tillery has captured George's spiritual odyssey, which enables us to take the journey with him to unlock the secrets, move aside the veil, and gain remarkable insight. An invaluable companion to his recent work on John Lennon, *The Cynical Idealist*."

> —**Bill Harry**, Founder of the Liverpool music publication,
> *Mersey Beat*

"One of the more fascinating among Beatles biographies, *Working Class Mystic* is neither hagiography nor rushed cash-in, but a richly informative account, understanding and empathetic. It is an insightful portrait of one of music's more complex characters and should be devoured by Harrison's devout disciples."

—**Joe Goodden**, author of *The Beatles Bible*

"Often referred to as the 'Quiet One,' George Harrison is given full voice in Gary Tillery's compact yet highly enlightening *Working Class Mystic*. Tillery nicely summarizes Harrison's life and music, framing the ex-Beatle's life in terms of his lifelong spiritual quest. One result of Harrison's search, which manifested itself as the seminal benefit rock concert known as the Concert for Bangladesh, is perhaps his greatest legacy. The sad ending of Harrison's life at such a young age and the life-threatening experience he and his wife Olivia faced at their home by a crazed intruder are leavened with the peace Harrison felt, even in the face of death. The music suggested for listening, Harrison's sense of humor, and his commitment to living in the spiritual world make this book ultimately uplifting and a great read."

—**Steve Matteo**, author of *Let It Be* and *Dylan*